THE LUCENT LIBRARY OF SCIENCE AND TECHNOLOGY

Computer Viruses

by Harry Henderson

LUCENT BOOKS

An imprint of Thomson Gale, a part of The Thomson Corporation

Detroit • New York • Sa_____ _____ _____ _____ Conn. _ Wate____, Ma___ ondon • Munich

For Lisa, whose creativity is infectious
(but only in a good way)

LIBRARY OF CONGRESS CATALOGING-IN-PUBLICATION DATA

Henderson, Harry, 1951–
  Computer viruses / by Harry Henderson.
    p. cm. — (Lucent library of science and technology)
  Includes bibliographical references and index.
  ISBN 1-59018-102-6 (hard cover : alk. paper)
  1. Computer viruses. I. Title. II. Series.
QA76.76.C68.H45 2005
005.8′4—dc22   2005013277

Printed in the United States of America

Table of Contents

Foreword   4

Introduction   7
Threats and Promises in the Information Age

Chapter 1   12
The Development of Computer Viruses

Chapter 2   29
The Worm Turns

Chapter 3   43
The Viruses Spread

Chapter 4   57
Why Do They Do It?

Chapter 5   68
Counting the Cost

Chapter 6   82
Fighting Back

Chapter 7   97
Viruses and the Future of Computing

Notes   109

Chronology   112

Glossary   114

For Further Reading   117

Works Consulted   120

Index   125

Picture Credits   128

About the Author   128

Foreword

"The world has changed far more in the past 100 years than in any other century in history. The reason is not political or economic, but technological—technologies that flowed directly from advances in basic science."

— Stephen Hawking, "A Brief History of Relativity," *Time*, 2000

The twentieth-century scientific and technological revolution that British physicist Stephen Hawking describes in the above quote has transformed virtually every aspect of human life at an unprecedented pace. Inventions unimaginable a century ago have not only become commonplace but are now considered necessities of daily life. As science historian James Burke writes, "We live surrounded by objects and systems that we take for granted, but which profoundly affect the way we behave, think, work, play, and in general conduct our lives."

For example, in just one hundred years, transportation systems have dramatically changed. In 1900 the first gasoline-powered motorcar had just been introduced, and only 144 miles of U.S. roads were hard-surfaced. Horse-drawn trolleys still filled the streets of American cities. The airplane had yet to be invented. Today 217 million vehicles speed along 4 million miles of U.S. roads. Humans have flown to the moon and commercial aircraft are capable of transporting passengers across the Atlantic Ocean in less than three hours.

The transformation of communications has been just as dramatic. In 1900 most Americans lived and worked on farms without electricity or mail delivery. Few people had ever heard a radio or spoken on a telephone. A hundred years later, 98 percent of American homes have telephones and televisions and more than 50 percent have personal computers. Some families even have more than one television and computer, and cell phones are now commonplace, even among the young. Data beamed from communication satellites routinely predict global weather conditions, and fiber-optic cable, e-mail, and the Internet have made worldwide telecommunication instantaneous.

Perhaps the most striking measure of scientific and technological change can be seen in medicine and public health. At the beginning of the twentieth century, the average American life span was forty-seven years. By the end of the century the average life span was approaching eighty years, thanks to advances in medicine including the development of vaccines and antibiotics, the discovery of powerful diagnostic tools such as X-rays, the lifesaving technology of cardiac and neonatal care, improvements in nutrition, and the control of infectious disease.

Rapid change is likely to continue throughout the twenty-first century as science reveals more about physical and biological processes such as global warming, viral replication, and electrical conductivity, and as people apply that new knowledge to personal decisions and government policy. Already, for example, an international treaty calls for immediate reductions in industrial and automobile emissions in response to studies that show a potentially dangerous rise in global temperatures is caused by human activity. Taking an active role in determining the direction of future changes depends on education; people must understand the possible uses of scientific research and the effects of the technology that surrounds them.

The Lucent Books Library of Science and Technology profiles key innovations and discoveries that have transformed the modern world. Each title strives to make a complex scientific discovery, technology, or phenomenon understandable and relevant to the reader. Because scientific discovery is rarely straightforward, each title explains the dead ends, fortunate accidents, and basic scientific methods by which the research into the subject proceeded. And every book examines the practical applications of an invention, branch of science, or scientific principle in industry, public health, and personal life, as well as potential future uses and effects based on ongoing research. Fully documented quotations, annotated bibliographies that include both print and electronic sources, glossaries, indexes, and technical illustrations are among the supplemental features designed to point researchers to further exploration of the subject.

Threats and Promises in the Information Age

Just about everyone has heard about computer viruses, those mysterious creatures that seem to be able to come in through cyberspace and infest the hard drives of personal computers (PCs). Viruses and their equally destructive cousins, worms, can make data disappear or bring whole networks of PCs to a grinding halt. Even worse, viruses spread by e-mail can trick people into revealing bank account numbers or passwords, leading to financial loss and even identity theft. Other forms of malicious software, or malware, can spy on Web browsing and send information to spammers and other online parasites.

The reason the threat of viruses and other cyber attacks is so important is that so much of the modern world's economic and even social life depends on computer systems and networks. These networks, for example, record billions of dollars worth of consumer purchases. They are vital for the operation of businesses, from corner pizza shops to huge multinational corporations. Other computers run the nation's electrical power supply, help control air traffic, and provide the information needed by every level of government. Whether the threat comes from teenage hackers seeking to break into a network just

A technician with an electric company monitors a sophisticated computer network that regulates energy use and distribution in a large city.

to prove they can, criminals looking to steal money, or committed terrorists wanting to cause disruption (or worse), protecting computer systems is vital to the nation's security and prosperity.

Meanwhile, the threats to computer networks appear to be getting more numerous. In 2003 the Computer Emergency Response Team (CERT) Coordination Center at Carnegie Mellon University reported 137,529 computer incidents, ranging from casual hacking attacks to major releases of computer viruses or worms. (This contrasts with only 252 incidents reported in 1990). By 2004 the increasing use of automated attack tools had created so many incidents that they could no longer be usefully counted. At the same time, the number of separate vulnerabilities reported in operating systems and software rose from 171 in 1995 to 3,780 in 2004. In other words, there are more holes in the defenses of the nation's computer systems, and more intruders seem to be getting in.

In part, the vulnerabilities that have made these widespread threats possible are the same technological advances that have made computers more useful and versatile. For example, being able to e-mail a photo with just a few clicks of a mouse also means that someone can e-mail a virus as an attachment. The ease in obtaining media files and software from Web sites and file-sharing services also means that viruses and programs called Trojan horses can enter, masquerading as desirable software. Software companies are always adding new features in an attempt to appeal to consumers, but these features are often exploited by ever-inventive hackers.

Technology, however, is only part of the story behind the explosion in computer viruses. In order to understand the battle between virus creators and the people whose job it is to protect computers, it is also necessary to look at the unique culture that they often share. It is a culture that prizes innovation over

*Infamous computer
hacker Kevin Mitnick,
who was convicted
of breaking into
secure business and
government computer
networks, is seen
here after his arrest
in 1995.*

conformity and that often sees laws and corporate
rules as obstacles that must be outsmarted or worked
around. The question then becomes whether people
who have gained a great deal of useful but potentially dangerous knowledge can exhibit a strong
sense of personal ethics to guide how they will use
what they have learned.

Because human responses to the opportunities (or temptations) that accompany advanced knowledge can vary, there is often no clear distinction between the kind of innovation that resulted in personal computers and the World Wide Web, and the kind of hacking that can damage computer networks and wreak havoc on the Web.

Indeed, even all self-described hackers are not the same: "white hats" try to expose and fix security flaws while "black hats" exploit them, with "gray hats" crossing and recrossing the moral line from one day to the next. Biographies of infamous teenage hackers show some, like Kevin Mitnick, going to prison but eventually turning their skills toward making computers better and safer, while others may remain in a shadowy underground.

Understanding the complex motives and choices involved in the development of computer viruses and countermeasures can help illuminate many other issues that arise in a society that is both empowered and made vulnerable by rapidly changing technology.

Finally, exploring the alarming but also intriguing exploits of virus makers and virus fighters raises important questions about the conflict between security and liberty that has so greatly preoccupied Americans since the terrorist attacks of September 11, 2001. For example, tighter controls on computer access and e-mail might make it easier to find and punish destructive hackers, but at a cost to everyone's privacy and ability to use technology freely. In the long run, the struggle to create a safer computer environment while continuing to enjoy freedom of expression and innovation will mirror the larger struggles for liberty and security that seem to be shaping the first years of the new century.

Chapter 1

The Development of Computer Viruses

The ideas that led to the first computer viruses are also at the heart of the development of modern computing. As computers became more versatile, they also became more vulnerable to manipulation. A brief look at how computers work and at their early history helps explain how viruses came into being in the first place.

The Virus Idea

During the 1940s, when the first electronic digital computers were being designed, there were three basic problems faced by computer engineers. They had to build the hardware—the circuits that store information and carry out instructions. Next, they had to decide how to write the instructions—or software—so the computer could understand them. Finally, they had to create ways to get data and instructions into the computer, process it, and get the results from the machine.

No matter what its purpose, the heart of a computer program is a set of instructions that tells the machine what to do with the data being fed into it. The basic instructions that can be carried out by a computer are actually rather simple. The machine can fetch data from memory or some external source such as a tape or disk. It can do calculations or perform logical tests such as determining whether one number is larger than another. The computer can also put data into memory or send it to some output device such as a printer.

In this 1947 photo, a technician performs maintenance on the massive ENIAC, the world's first digital computer.

The earliest computers and automatic calculators read in one program instruction at a time, carried it out, read the next instruction, and so on. However,

John Mauchly, one of ENIAC's inventors, programs the computer to solve a mathematical problem.

when they were designing ENIAC, generally considered to be the first electronic digital computer, mathematician John von Neumann and inventors John Presper Eckert and John Mauchly developed an idea that would make computers far more flexible.

Instead of retrieving, executing, and discarding instructions one at a time, the whole program would be loaded and stored in memory.

This stored-program concept meant that a computer could go back to previously executed instructions, executing them over and over again until some specified condition was met. Programs could also instruct computers to make decisions. That is, they could execute instructions in the form of "If (something is true) do this; otherwise, do that."

In 1949, however, von Neumann described another important consequence of the stored-program idea. Once the program is stored in the computer, the program instructions look just like data, because they are both in the form of binary numbers—that is, numbers that consist of strings of zeros and ones. Whether a number such as 11010110 stored in a particular location in computer memory is an instruction or some data to be processed has nothing to do with the number itself, but depends on its intended use and perhaps its location in the computer's memory.

Therefore, there is nothing to stop someone from writing a program that enters the computer's memory disguised as data. Von Neumann pointed out that a program could make a copy of itself. The copy, when run, would make another copy, and so on. This is the basic principle that would be used later by computer worms that copy themselves into whatever memory or disk space they can find, whether on their home machine or some other computer on a network.

Mainframes—A Sterile Environment

Although self-reproducing programs are at the heart of computer worms and viruses, the computing environment was not yet very favorable for them to thrive. The first computers, such as the room-filling ENIAC and its successors such as UNIVAC and the early IBM mainframes of the 1950s, were run by professional operators who worked either directly for the company that owned the computer or sometimes for the manufacturer. They worked in closed, air-conditioned rooms isolated from the world at large.

Computers were not connected to one another or to the outside world. Only people with direct access had the means of programming the machine or entering data. To run a program, a deck of punched cards or a tape had to be fed into the machine. These cards or tapes contained instructions that told the computer how to perform calculations and where to move data around in the machine's memory. They also contained the data to be worked with, such as payroll records or scientific measurements. After going through the programmed steps, the computer would typically output another tape or stack of cards with the results or possibly print a report.

Thus, there was no way for someone to sneak in an unwanted program and no place inside the machine to conceal some small, mischievous set of instructions. And with computers so large and expensive that only big businesses and government agencies could afford them, it was unlikely that maverick programmers would get access to them.

Minicomputers and the First Hackers

New developments in electronics technology and computer design soon made greater access possible. In 1957 Kenneth Olsen, an engineer who had helped build the huge computers known as mainframes for IBM, felt that the giant company had become too set in its ways of doing business. In response, Olsen started Digital Equipment Corporation (DEC). His goal was to develop new uses for transistors to create smaller computer components. The result of Olsen's experiments was the PDP-1, which DEC brought out in 1960. This was the first commercial minicomputer.

Although the PDP-1 could not process data as quickly as a mainframe, the whole computer fit into

Ken Olsen founded Digital Equipment Corporation (DEC) in 1957. DEC produced the PDP-1, one of the first commercially available minicomputers.

a case about the size of a home refrigerator. Also, the machine cost $120,000—a lot of money at the time, but much less than the cost of a million-dollar mainframe. This meant that smaller companies and many academic departments within colleges and universities could now afford a computer of their own. The number of computers—and access to them—thus began to expand enormously.

With the growing numbers of computers came an increased need for people to program and run them. Whereas owners of mainframes paid IBM or other manufacturers for the necessary software and its maintenance, purchasers of minicomputers made do with little more than a rudimentary operating system and a skimpy technical manual. Owners, such as university computing departments, created their own software to make the machines do something useful.

In this freewheeling environment, typical of computer science departments at institutions like the Massachusetts Institute of Technology (MIT) or Stanford University, people who could write clever, effective programs were welcomed, or at least tolerated. This was true even if they were merely talented students or had no official connection with the department that owned the machine. Twelve-year-old Peter Deutsch, for example, hung around MIT's computer

Hacker Talk

Like any in-group, hackers have developed their own lingo. It includes special forms of spelling as well as a unique vocabulary. Here are some examples:

hacktivism: Hacking for a social cause, such as posting protest messages on corporate or government Web sites.

lamer: A wannabe hacker

leet or **133t:** Elite, showing top-notch hacking skills

phile: File

warez: Software (usually illegally copied)

white hat: A hacker who is interested in gaining knowledge rather than damaging systems.

In their writing, hackers often substitute *ph* for *f*, as in *phreak*, a usage dating back to the original phone phreaks who hacked the telephone network starting in the 1970s. Hackers also like to substitute numbers for the letters they resemble: Thus, *leet* becomes *133t*, and this way of writing is also called 133t sp34k (leet speak).

room, talked his way onto its prototype TX-O microcomputer, and was soon correcting the programming mistakes of graduate students twice his age.

At MIT, fascinated by the possibilities of the machine, the hackers, as these informal visitors were known, often stayed up all night in order to get a chance to work with the TX-O and later its more powerful successors. One hacker even took to sleeping by day in a makeshift nest inside an air conditioning duct, to emerge only at night when he saw the computer was not being used. By the early 1960s, the hackers were generating computer music, sending blips of light careening across a cathode-ray tube (CRT) screen in Spacewars, the first video game, and rigging up keyboards to use for data entry in place of punched tapes.

The most important innovation to which hackers contributed, though, was probably the software that allowed time-sharing—the ability to share a computer among several users, each running his or her own program. As it came from the manufacturer, this time-sharing software was balky and unreliable, but the hackers quickly developed and distributed their own versions that ran more smoothly.

The hackers' ideas reflected an attitude that was different from that found at the computer companies. Unlike the world of the manufacturers, where software was a product to be tightly controlled and sold for a profit, the hacker world saw software as a resource to be shared freely and modified as needed. In other words, software development was a communal effort. As writer Steven Levy later observed:

Hackers believe that essential lessons can be learned about the systems—about the world—from taking things apart, seeing how they work, and using this knowledge to create new and even more interesting things. They resent any person, physical barrier, or law that tries to keep them from doing this. . . . All information should be free.[1]

As university computing departments grew, however, they began to see a greater need for rules. Administrators began to crack down on unauthorized use of machines and introduced security measures such as requiring users to log on with a name and password. Hackers disdained such rules, however, and found ways to bypass security.

One of the favorite means for bypassing security was a fairly simple ruse. A program could be written that put up a display that looked just like the regular log-in screen. When the program was left running on a terminal, an authorized user (perhaps an administrator) might walk up and type in his or her password. The program would then indicate that the computer had crashed—a frequent-enough occurrence in those days—and the user would leave to seek help in solving the problem. The user's password, however, had actually been recorded by the hacker's program and stored in a file for later use.

The original hackers generally had no desire to use such tactics to harm computers or to steal from people. However, the combination of intimate knowledge of how computers work and the ability to trick less knowledgeable people would prove tempting to others as the use of computers began to spread through the business and academic worlds.

Core Wars

A key advantage of the time-sharing introduced with minicomputers is that it allowed for multitasking, or the ability of a computer to run more than one program at a time. The central processing unit (CPU) could run one program for a tiny fraction of a second, then turn its attention to the next program stored in memory, and so on. Because the processor switched its attention from program to program so quickly, to the user it seemed like all the programs were running at the same time.

In a computer where there are many programs sharing the same memory, however, the operating system must be careful to make sure that one program cannot intrude into the memory being used by another program. If such a collision occurs, then the other program may start using information not intended for it. And if the computer's instructions are garbled in this way, the program will malfunction or even stop running. The ability of a program to place instructions in another program—intentional or not—is the key to creating a computer virus. The

Computer hackers are part of a rebellious subculture of highly skilled and extremely competitive computer programmers.

first appearance of this behavior, however, was in the form of a harmless but intriguing game.

In 1984 *Scientific American* published a feature article by A.K. Dewdney about a computer game called Core Wars that had become a fascinating test of skill for programmers. Unlike most computer games that are played *on* a computer, Core Wars was played *in* a computer. Using a special computer language called Redcode, participants designed programs that would try to "punch holes" in other competitors' programs that shared the same simulated computer memory and also try to repair any damage they sustained. (*Core* referred to an early type of magnetic computer memory.) The "bullets" fired by these battling programs were essentially nonsense data that would be substituted for other programs' instructions.

Core Wars was played in a sort of virtual arena inside a computer, and the warring programs thus could not harm the computer system or spread to other computers. However, many of the ideas of Core Wars—such as having programs try to fill memory with their own code while probing for vulnerable areas of memory—would soon be adopted to create computer worms and viruses.

A Virus Experiment

By the 1970s, advances in both hardware and software meant that sophisticated computers were available to thousands of university students, scientists, and other researchers. In particular, an operating system—the basic software that allows the various parts of a computer to work together—known as Unix allowed dozens of programs to perform a great variety of tasks simultaneously on the increasingly powerful minicomputers. The typical university system would have many users who could connect to a shared computer over telephone lines.

In 1983 a University of Southern California researcher named Fred Cohen was concerned that

these popular shared computer systems were vulnerable to being hijacked by destructive programs introduced by malicious or careless users. He designed an experiment to see whether such a program could be introduced into a computer system without even experienced users and administrators being able to detect it. As the program was being developed, a colleague dubbed it a "virus." The virus was inserted into a new Unix program that appeared to be one of the many other programs used for tasks such as sorting files or finding text. Many users ran the program to see what it would do, and unknown to them, the virus gained access to their private files.

Unix allowed users to connect simultaneously to a single server. By the 1980s, as shown here, French users were connecting to a network called Minitel.

The experimental virus was carefully designed so that it could not escape to other systems, and files were promptly disinfected with no lasting harm to users. However, the experiment yielded several disturbing results. What was perhaps most alarming was that the virus was able to find its way quickly to even the most highly secured parts of the system, including the special files used by system administrators to keep track of user accounts.

The fact that the virus was spread by enticing users with something interesting (a new program) suggested that human psychology would make it easy for ill-intended persons to gain similar access. Yet the experimenters met with great resistance from the system administrators, who generally denied that their systems were truly vulnerable. Despite the possible danger that malicious people could create destructive types of viruses, the administrators generally refused to improve their security systems or to develop ways to detect and neutralize viruses.

PCs and the First "Wild" Viruses

Even as Cohen and other researchers were studying the potential of viruses to infect minicomputer systems, an even smaller machine known as a personal computer (PC) was starting to appear in businesses, homes, and schools. PCs were less powerful and sophisticated than minicomputers, but they were easier to use and cheap enough for just about anyone to buy.

Users of PCs needed to know little or nothing about programming their machines. They inserted floppy disks containing the programs into the computer, and these told the machine to work as a word processor or organize data in a way that anyone—a store clerk checking inventory or an accountant working with a business's balance sheet, for example —could use. Before it was able to run a program of this sort—known as an application—the computer had to load its operating software, usually called a disk operating system (DOS). This, too, could be provided on a floppy disk.

Around 1982, a fifteen-year-old high school student named Richard Skrenta wrote the first PC virus for the Apple II, one of the most popular early PCs. He called it Elk Cloner. The virus was created in a modified copy of the DOS stored on a floppy disk. When a user inserted the disk, the operating system loaded into memory and appeared to work normally.

However, the virus included instructions that would be activated when a disk was put into the drive. Any new disks put in the drive would be scanned by the virus, and if they contained the normal operating

In the early 1980s, many teenagers became talented computer programmers. A few, however, began creating some of the first PC viruses.

Software Piracy

Makers of commercial software face a fundamental problem. While it may take hundreds of thousands of dollars to develop a business program or even a game, making a copy of a disk or CD costs only a few dollars at most. In the early days of personal computing, software was relatively more expensive than it is today, while many users (often teenagers) had little money. The temptation to copy software and distribute or swap it was hard to resist.

Software companies responded by using various forms of copy protection to make it harder to reproduce disks. A number of hackers, sometimes called software pirates, soon cracked the copy protection and distributed the disks at computer swap meets, on bulletin boards, and later, on the Internet.

Pirating commercial software, music, or movies is illegal, and industry groups have sometimes sued pirates, file swappers, and even users. Besides involving legal risk, downloading pirated software, or warez, also carries the risk that the files contain viruses or spyware.

system, that would be replaced by the version that included the virus. This meant that if the infected disk was shared with another user, it would infect that user's DOS disks as well. Since many users swapped software, the virus began to spread.

The Elk Cloner virus did not actually harm users' data. Every fiftieth time an infected disk was inserted it displayed the following poem on the screen:

Elk Cloner: The program with a personality
    It will get on all your disks
    It will infiltrate your chips
    Yes it's Cloner!

It will stick to you like glue
    It will modify ram too
    Send in the Cloner![2]

At the worst, Elk Cloner was merely an annoying way of forcing people to read bad poetry. However, it was a taste of worse things to come.

Viruses Come of Age

By the mid-1980s, the IBM PC and similar machines made by other companies were being widely used in business; all used versions of the same operating system, called MS-DOS or PC-DOS. Having millions of machines available that could all run the same software encouraged the efforts of virus writers who wanted to become famous—or infamous.

The first IBM PC virus, Brain, was written in 1986 and worked in a way similar to Elk Cloner. One difference was that the IBM PC included a feature that allowed small programs to be stored in memory along with the main application program. This

Early computer viruses were spread by floppy disks such as the disks these school children are holding up in this photo from 1986.

stay-resident feature allowed the creation of many useful utility programs (such as a pop-up notepad or phone dialer), but it also provided a place for viruses to hide. The Brain virus, like Elk Cloner, spread by floppy disks. When an infected disk was used to start (boot) the system, the virus ran and installed itself in memory, where it could copy itself to other disks as they were inserted.

Early viruses such as Brain and Elk Cloner were easy to detect and remove by means of special antivirus programs. However, coming years quickly brought more sophisticated PC viruses. Viruses such as Suriv-02 (*Suriv* is *virus* spelled backward) began to find other ways to infect PCs. Instead of targeting the part of the disk containing the operating system, they began to infect other programs. Other viruses began to use encryption to disguise their instructions so they could not be recognized by the antivirus programs.

By the late 1980s, PC viruses had finally become recognized as a threat by the software industry. IBM even set up a special laboratory to check its software for viruses before it was distributed. However, most users could remain safe from infection as long as they only used disks from reputable sources. This was about to change. The connecting of computers to networks would soon give viruses a way to spread thousands of times more quickly.

Chapter 2

The Worm
Turns

As late as 1975, computer worms and viruses mostly were the stuff of fiction, like John Brunner's novel, *Shockwave Rider*. In Brunner's novel, the hero uses a program called a tapeworm to disable a computer network being used by a totalitarian government to control the citizenry. At the time the novel was written, computer networks were in their infancy. Only a small number of researchers were linking their computers together to make the exchange of information easier. But as networks expanded, the threat posed by worms—small programs that can replicate themselves unaided—grew as well.

By the early 1980s, computer networks (including an early form of the Internet) were increasingly found at universities and private research labs. Furthermore, at the Xerox Palo Alto Research Center, researchers John Shock and Jon Hepps had begun to develop actual worm programs that could travel around the network. These worms were intended to perform helpful tasks. The town crier worm, for example, could post announcements on users' terminals. A more sophisticated worm, dubbed the "vampire," was designed to run late at night, when most of the computers were idle. It would find "sleeping" computers and parcel out complex calculations to them, enabling the machines to do useful work while their owners were not using them.

Early on, however, the Xerox researchers learned that worms could get out of control. One night a worm containing a programming error crashed every computer on the network. The next morning, each time anyone attempted to restart a machine, a worm immediately crashed it again. The researchers had to write a special program to block the rogue worms. Such experimental worms were really only of interest to computer scientists. But a few years later, a worm would make headlines and raise fears about the security of the nation's growing computer infrastructure.

Worms on the Internet

In the late 1980s, most Americans had not heard about the Internet, but the growing network had now become an important part of life in the scientific community. Thousands of engineers, scientists, and university students used e-mail and other services on the network every day, and many posted messages on Usenet, a sort of giant electronic bulletin board. Most of the computers used in this environment were not the desktop computers used in offices and in the home, but more powerful minicomputer systems such as the VAX made by DEC and workstations made by Sun.

Still, these computers proved to be just as vulnerable as their smaller cousins. On the night of November 2, 1988, something strange began to happen to computers in universities and research labs across the United States. Programs began to run more and more slowly, sometimes grinding to a halt. E-mail stopped flowing. Shortly after midnight, a manager named Andy Sudduth at Harvard University posted a message on Usenet that read "There may be a virus loose on the Internet."[3]

By dawn, researchers at the University of California, Berkeley and MIT were working feverishly to isolate the mysterious program. They soon suspected that a worm rather than a virus had been loosed on the Net. That suspicion was fueled by the fact that the rogue program appeared to be able to reproduce itself without the aid of any software in the computers it entered. Because there were now thousands of linked computers, this gave the worm the potential to cause widespread disruption.

Although the researchers now knew some of its characteristics, tracking down this worm was not easy. Later, they discovered that it had numerous ways to

By the 1980s, most university researchers were using computers as research tools. These scientists are reviewing the results of computer models of atmospheric change.

Virtual Communities

According to the popular stereotype, the inventors of new computer hardware and software are nerds who are obsessed with technology and neglect to have any sort of social life. Like all stereotypes, this can be partly true. Certainly mastering the complicated details of modern technology can require endless hours of painstaking study and experimentation. A personality capable of such concentration might also be more prone to becoming obsessed and socially isolated. Many classic hackers fit into this mold.

However, many of the most successful computer scientists (such as those who created the Internet and World Wide Web) have also been interested in how people communicate and interact. Further, the Unix operating system that took hold in universities beginning in the 1970s was particularly well-designed for the development of a community of programmers. Unix encourages programmers to create new tools and utilities that can be combined with existing functions to create useful scripts and programs. Meanwhile, the development of Usenet (later called Netnews) enabled users to post messages on hundreds of different topics—among them, computer security and strategies for dealing with threats such as worms and viruses.

Social philosopher Howard Rheingold created the term *virtual community* to describe how people can work together online and form lasting relationships. Today's forms of virtual communities can include conferencing systems such as the Well, newsgroups, chat rooms, Web logs, and elaborate online game worlds such as *Second Life*.

cover up its tracks. For example, it disabled the computer's core-dump function that normally allowed users to examine everything that was in the machine's memory at the time of a crash. Further, when it was finished executing, the worm tried to delete files that recorded its activity and even to delete itself. This all meant that in effect, the dead worm left no corpse to be examined. Finally the worm could fork, or spawn new copies of itself, and then delete the original, making it harder to trace its source.

Refusing to give up, the researchers shared ideas by news postings and e-mail as they struggled to contain the spreading infection. Thus, the same network that was being crippled by the worm was proving its value by helping people pool information and suggestions for halting its spread—though the slow-down of many machines was also hampering communications.

Anatomy of the Worm

As researchers studied the rogue program, they began to piece together how it worked—and how to stop it from spreading. Unlike Windows and other PC operating systems in use at the time, the Unix operating system used on minicomputers and workstations was specifically designed for users and programs to be able to communicate easily with one another, whether on the same machine or across the country.

For example, the Unix finger utility enabled one to find out whether another user was logged in to the network, as well as allowing one to learn other information the user offered to the public, such as an address or phone number. The finger facility is provided by a "daemon" program that runs continuously, waiting for information requests.

The finger program, however, had a flaw. It assumed that it would receive only a small amount of information, such as the log-in ID of a user. This information is stored in a small area of memory called a buffer. Unfortunately for the Internet users, finger (and some other Unix programs) did not check an incoming piece of information to make sure it was not too long to fit in the buffer. When such an oversize string of code arrived, that extra information would then replace parts of the computer's memory. By carefully constructing this information, a malicious programmer could insert his or her own commands and take control of the system.

Another flaw being exploited by the intruder was found in sendmail, the Unix program that handles the routing and delivery of e-mail. This program includes special debugging routines that allow the program to be tested by sending it commands instead of mail addresses. However, this also meant that someone using the right commands could take control of the mail system.

Once it had been installed on a machine connected to a network, the worm opened the file containing users' passwords. Although the passwords were encrypted, it was fairly easy for the worm to try encrypting various common words and combinations of letters and compare the results to the encrypted passwords. When a match was found, the worm could gain access to that account—and some of those accounts provided access to still other machines on the network.

Once the worm had access to another machine, it could use the finger or sendmail functions or an-

A Good Worm?

The first computer worms developed by researchers were intended to perform useful tasks. Some experts ask if good worms might be used to fight bad ones. Others respond that while this is an intriguing idea, it may not be a good plan. For example, one unknown author created a worm called Welchia. This worm was supposed to spread from machine to machine, automatically downloading and installing a Microsoft code patch intended to disable the destructive Blaster worm. Unfortunately, the author of Welchia had not anticipated what would happen to Microsoft's Web site when it received thousands of download requests per hour. As a result, other users trying to access the Microsoft site were virtually locked out.

Although someday carefully designed beneficial worms might be a practical way to respond to malicious software, a safer and more practical alternative is to use the automatic update features provided with many modern operating systems and software suites. With automatic updates, the system checks the software company's Web site regularly (perhaps once a week) to see if there are any patches to download.

other facility called remote execution to copy a small vector program to the second machine and start running it. In turn, the vector program would establish a connection back to the original machine and obtain a copy of the rest of the worm. The worm had now reproduced.

Out of Control

Besides trying to understand the worm and stop it from spreading, researchers also wanted to know who had created it. They did not have to wait very long to find out. The worm's author, Robert Tappan Morris Jr., was a computer science student who had devised the worm as what he thought would be a harmless experiment. (Morris's father was a renowned cryptographer who, ironically, had devised the system for encrypting Unix passwords, a key system function that his son's worm would exploit.)

While Morris had wanted his worm to spread, he apparently had not intended for it to seriously

In 1990 Robert Morris Jr. was convicted of violating federal law by releasing a virus he wrote onto the Internet.

impair any systems or the Internet itself. He had tried to set things up so that the worm would generally not make another copy of itself on a given machine if a copy was already running there. Once established, the worm would set a special flag variable that could be checked by other worms. If the flag were set, then any additional worms were supposed to self-destruct six out of seven times. Thus, the worm would spread relatively slowly, and with at most only a few copies per machine, the operation of the computer would not be slowed significantly.

However, because of a delay between the worm's checking the flag and its self-destructing, worms often began to reproduce and fill up a machine faster than they could be destroyed. In turn, as the machine filled with worms, access to the special flag often became blocked, preventing the worms from getting the signal to self-destruct. Meanwhile, the accumulating worms busily looked for connections so they could spread to other machines.

Morris soon learned that his worm was swamping the Internet. However, he hesitated for hours before telling anyone, later confessing that he was afraid of what might happen if he admitted that he was the worm's author. Meanwhile, *New York Times* reporter John Markoff learned of Morris's likely involvement in the worm attack and began to write about it in a series of front-page stories. By then, the distribution of patches for the vulnerable Unix utilities and instructions to system administrators had eradicated the worm from the network, and operations had returned to normal.

Aftermath

Even though long-term damage was minimal, the worm of 1988 had considerable impact on the growing community of Internet users. By temporarily knocking out about a tenth of the sixty thousand computer systems connected to the Internet, the worm showed how much people were beginning to depend on computer networks. The worm attack also, as writers Katie Hafner and John Markoff noted, "engaged people who knew nothing about computers but who were worried about how this new technology could be used for criminal ends."[4]

In response to the attack, the Defense Advanced Research Project Administration, the government agency that administered the Internet at the time, established the Computer Emergency Response Team (CERT) at Carnegie Mellon University. This was the first organization specifically set up to coordinate information about and response to computer attacks.

The worm incident also prompted considerable thinking about the risks associated with computer technology and the ethical standards to be applied to it. As Unix expert Eugene Spafford noted in his technical report on the worm:

> This whole episode should prompt us to think about the ethics and laws concerning access to computers. The technology we use has developed so quickly it is not always easy to determine where the proper boundaries of moral action should be. . . . I believe it is critical to realize that such behavior is clearly inappropriate now. Entire businesses are now dependent, wisely or not, on the undisturbed functioning of computers. Many people's careers, property, and lives may be placed in jeopardy by acts of computer sabotage and mischief.[5]

By the 1990s, computers played an essential role in the daily tasks of most office workers, such as these investment bankers and traders.

As for Robert Tappan Morris Jr., he was convicted of violating the 1986 federal Computer Fraud and Abuse Act. In 1991 he was sentenced to three years of probation, four hundred hours of community service, and a $10,000 fine, far short of the maximum penalty of five years in prison and a $250,000 fine. While some observers wanted a tougher sentence to deter future computer attacks, others noted that Morris's worm did not actually result in the loss of any data, though it did use up staff time and temporarily deprive users of access to their systems.

Worms on the Desktop

Eugene Spafford ended his report on the Internet worm with the prediction that the lessons learned

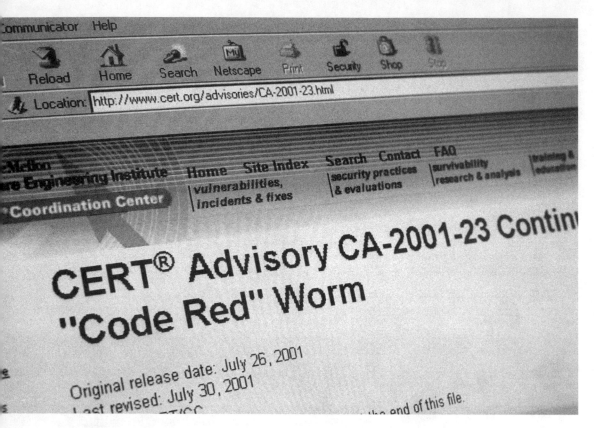

Communicator   Help

Reload   Home   Search   Netscape   Print   Security   Shop   Stop

Location: http://www.cert.org/advisories/CA-2001-23.html

Mellon
re Engineering Institute   Home   Site Index   Search   Contact   FAQ
                          vulnerabilities,   security practices   survivability   training &
Coordination Center   incidents & fixes   & evaluations   research & analysis   education

CERT® Advisory CA-2001-23 Contin
"Code Red" Worm

Original release date: July 26, 2001
Last revised: July 30, 2001

the end of this file.

The Computer Emergency Response Team (CERT) at Carnegie Mellon University posted this advisory warning about the Code Red Internet worm on July 30, 2001.

would lead to better security and that there would be no further incidents. That proved to be too optimistic, although vigorous action by the Unix community was able to fix many of the flaws exploited by later worms infecting personal computers.

By the 1990s, personal computers had become a vital part of everyday life. Increasingly, these machines, which ran sophisticated versions of Microsoft Windows, were connected to local networks and to the Internet. By the middle of the decade, the World Wide Web and Web browsing software were bringing the Internet to millions of desktop computers in offices, schools, and homes. This connectivity, together with a number of flaws in operating systems and software, created a fertile environment for the growth of viruses, worms, and other forms of malicious software.

A New Generation of Worms

The increasing sophistication and power of PCs was matched by the inventiveness of those who created worms. While the earliest worms generally exploited flaws in basic utilities, newer worms often targeted the increasingly sophisticated services offered by the Windows operating system and by office software.

In 2001 the Code Red and Nimda (*admin* spelled backwards) worms spread quickly by exploiting flaws in Microsoft Web Server and Internet Explorer software. A later worm, called SQL Slammer, exploited a different vulnerability in SQL Server, a facility that processes database requests over the Internet. Each time a vulnerability was exposed, Microsoft would respond by making a patch available. Conscientious Windows users learned to run Windows Update regularly to download the seemingly endless succession of patches that Microsoft's software developers distributed in response to each newly discovered vulnerability.

The creators of worms responded in kind. By 2003 a new wave of smarter, more prolific worms was being loosed onto the Internet. Sobig.F, a worm that spread itself from machine to machine by way of a user's e-mail address book, reached the point where one in seventeen e-mails sent each day were from the worm. Mail servers staggered under the load, and some institutions such as the *New York Times* briefly shut down the e-mail service to protect their systems.

But Sobig had another feature that was even more troubling. Security experts who examined the code discovered that the worm included instructions that would enable it to contact twenty secret Web sites, from which it could download additional instructions that had been left there by its author. In effect, Sobig could continually change its code and add new capabilities, keeping itself ahead of attempts to create patches. Fortunately for the network community, virus fighters succeeded in identifying nineteen of the twenty sites and disabling them before the worms could "phone home" for instructions, while the twentieth site turned out to be inactive.

While worms exploited flaws in operating systems and software, viruses, too, were continuing to evolve. Like worms, viruses would find in the rapidly growing Internet an ideal growth medium.

Chapter 3

The Viruses Spread

The ability of worms to reproduce automatically by exploiting flaws in operating systems and software was alarming enough to computer security experts. By the 1990s, three conditions were creating a fertile environment for the spread of computer viruses: widespread use of e-mail, new ways to trigger viruses, and the arrival of millions of new users who knew little about the operation and vulnerability of computer systems. This environment allowed viruses to take advantage of the network's weakest link: the individual user.

You've Got Virus

In March 1999, millions of computer users opened their e-mail and saw a message in the inbox with the subject header "Important Message." The message itself had a number of variants. One read: "Here is that document you asked for . . . don't show anyone else ;-)." The message was accompanied by a little icon indicating that there was a document attached. When the user double clicked to open the document, it loaded into Microsoft Word.

The message appeared to be a list of passwords for pornographic Web sites. Whether tempted or irritated,

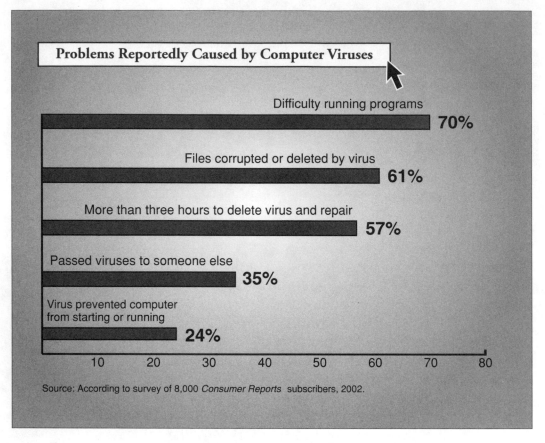

Problems Reportedly Caused by Computer Viruses

Difficulty running programs
70%

Files corrupted or deleted by virus
61%

More than three hours to delete virus and repair
57%

Passed viruses to someone else
35%

Virus prevented computer
from starting or running
24%

10   20   30   40   50   60   70   80

Source: According to survey of 8,000 *Consumer Reports* subscribers, 2002.

the user might spend some time thinking about whether to go to one of the Web sites or perhaps to send an indignant response to whoever had sent the e-mail.

However, the attachment also contained something extra that was invisible to the user but destructive in its effects. Microsoft Word and a number of other Windows programs had the ability to run small add-on programs called macros. Such programs were intended to be included in documents to help with formatting documents or other tasks. However, where there could be a program, there could be a virus—in this case, a virus called Melissa.

While the user was thinking about what to do, the virus inside the attachment was busy seeking a way to reproduce. Exploiting a flaw in the Microsoft Outlook mail program, the virus could retrieve the first fifty e-mail addresses from the user's address book. Soon the virus was mailing copies of itself (attached to a copy of the message) to those fifty computer users.

The Melissa virus was one of the fastest-spreading viruses in computer history. Although it did little damage to users' data, the e-mail it generated could

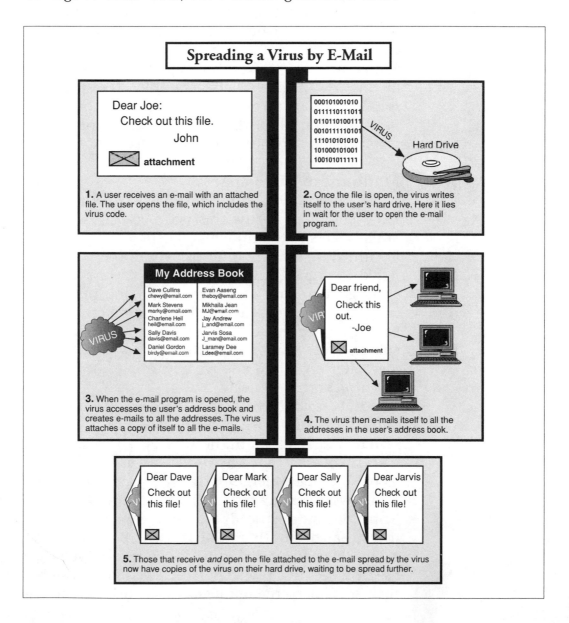

Spreading a Virus by E-Mail

Dear Joe:
Check out this file.
John

☒ attachment

1. A user receives an e-mail with an attached file. The user opens the file, which includes the virus code.

000101001010
011111011101l
0110110100111
0010111110101
1110101010l0
101000101001
100101011111

VIRUS

Hard Drive

2. Once the file is open, the virus writes itself to the user's hard drive. Here it lies in wait for the user to open the e-mail program.

My Address Book

Dave Cullins
chewy@email.com

Evan Aaseng
theboy@email.com

Mark Stevens
marky@email.com

Mikhaila Jean
MJ@email.com

Charlene Heil
heil@email.com

Jay Andrew
j_and@email.com

Sally Davis
davis@email.com

Jarvis Sosa
J_man@email.com

Daniel Gordon
birdy@email.com

Laramey Dee
Ldee@email.com

VIRUS

3. When the e-mail program is opened, the virus accesses the user's address book and creates e-mails to all the addresses. The virus attaches a copy of itself to all the e-mails.

Dear friend,
Check this out.
-Joe

☒ attachment

VIRUS

4. The virus then e-mails itself to all the addresses in the user's address book.

Dear Dave
Check out this file!
☒

Dear Mark
Check out this file!
☒

Dear Sally
Check out this file!
☒

Dear Jarvis
Check out this file!
☒

5. Those that receive *and* open the file attached to the e-mail spread by the virus now have copies of the virus on their hard drive, waiting to be spread further.

clog mail servers and slow down other systems. Fortunately, the federal government's newly formed CERT and the leading private antivirus software companies were ready to spring into action. Soon updates for antivirus programs were in wide distribution, allowing Melissa to be removed from infected systems.

A further sort of inoculation against the infection occurred when a new word of advice was widely circulated by the mass media and by local system administrators: "Do not open unknown e-mail attachments." Since Melissa could only spread if someone opened the attachment, users could prevent infection simply by deleting e-mails containing suspicious-looking attachments.

Manhunt in Cyberspace

Through the 1990s, viruses like Melissa became ever more common. Partly, this was because computer virus writers felt confident that they would not be identified by security officials, whom they often referred to disparagingly as "suits" or "drones." However, government and corporate concerns about computer viruses were growing, and determination among authorities to punish their creators was hardening. At the same time, virus hunters were becoming better organized and were learning how to analyze attacks more quickly.

In the case of Melissa, the Windows operating system itself had helped identify the culprit. One researcher, Richard Smith, head of Phar Lap Software, had discovered that Microsoft was using a unique global user identifier, or GUID, for each copy of the Windows operating system. This identifier was being embedded automatically in any computer code the user created. Smith found the GUID in the executable code for Melissa and posted it on a Web page used by security researchers. A Swedish researcher then recognized the number as also appearing in an-

Computer programmer David L. Smith pleaded guilty on December 9, 1999, to creating and distributing the Melissa virus, which disabled the e-mail networks of many large companies.

other virus, called VicodinES (whimsically named for a powerful painkiller).

Smith also noticed that the automatic log kept by the software development system used to create Melissa had recorded certain names as the virus code was being created and revised. One such name was David L. Smith. Richard Smith (who was no relation to David) forwarded this information to the FBI. Meanwhile, another team of virus hunters, working independently on behalf of the Internet service provider America Online, had identified a David L. Smith as the person who had first posted a copy of Melissa on the Web.

Armed with this user information and an address, federal investigators obtained and executed a search warrant on Smith's apartment, and Smith was arrested a few hours later. He eventually pleaded guilty in exchange for a relatively light sentence of twenty months in prison, a five-thousand-dollar fine, and a hundred hours of community service. Although the virus had cost users an estimated $80 million, authorities justified the lenient treatment by saying that Smith had given them information that could be used to thwart future attacks by other virus creators.

The Love Bug

Melissa was followed by other viruses that were similar in the way they worked. One particularly destructive example was the Love Bug virus, so-called because the e-mails it sent had "I love you" in their subject line. Indeed, this use of the subject line was the only really clever feature of the virus. Everyone, it seems, can use some love, and an e-mail with an attached love note was hard to resist. (Opening the attachment, of course, launched the bug's code.) The resulting damage in terms of computer slowdowns, lost working time, and diversion of employees has been estimated at several billion dollars.

As with Melissa, the Love Bug's code held clues to the identity of its perpetrator, who turned out to be Onel de Guzman, a twenty-three-year-old computer science student at the AMA Computer College in the Philippines. Later, a college thesis proposal by de Guzman was unearthed. The proposal included a program, intended to harvest Internet accounts, that closely resembled the Love Bug.

Unlike Melissa's creator, the Love Bug's author could not be arrested, because at the time the Philippines had no law against distributing computer viruses. Indeed, one of the most frustrating factors for law enforcers is that a growing number of viruses

This computer screen shows an e-mail inbox filled with messages containing the Love Bug virus, which shut down computer networks around the world.

and worms come from countries (particularly in Eastern Europe, Russia, and Asia) where laws against computer crime are nonexistent or poorly enforced.

March of the Zombies

Viruses such as Melissa and the Love Bug took advantage of computer networks to spread from one machine to another, but the targets were the computers themselves. By the early twenty-first century, however, it had occurred to virus creators to harness the capabilities of the computers they infected. These

Using a Virus to Attack a Web Site

Coordinated attacks against a Web site can shut down access to that site, resulting in lost time online and possible lost revenues for commercial Web sites.

1. Numerous computers are infected by a virus containing attack instructions. The virus is dormant at first. Users have normal access to the target Web site.

2. At a predetermined time, the infected computers, following the virus instructions, bombard the target Web site with information requests. If there are too many requests, the target system slows down.

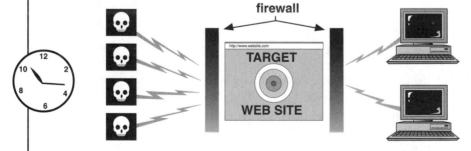

3. As the attack continues, the target system may have to shut down access completely. The Web site can no longer provide service to its users. With a commercial site this means loss of business and revenue.

= Attacker   = User

machines could in turn be used to launch massive attacks on a targeted company or government agency.

Suppose, for example, a hacker wants to attack and shut down a Web site. One way to do this is to create a virus or worm that can spread to thousands of PCs, such as by e-mail. In addition to just copying itself, however, the virus includes special instructions that tell it to use its host computer's Internet connection to send repeated information requests to the target site. Starting at a preset time, thousands or perhaps millions of virus-infected computers begin to blast the target site with requests, drastically slowing its ability to respond to legitimate requests, in the end effectively shutting it down. The virus has in essence created an army of unwilling "zombie" computers and used it against the target.

In 2003 the author of the Blaster worm set up just such an attack, aimed at Microsoft Corporation's software update site. This attack was potentially serious, because Windows users depend on this site to be able to download the latest security fixes for preventing viruses and worms from taking advantage of flaws in the operating system and other Microsoft software.

At the height of the attack, about four hundred thousand zombie computers were launching the Web requests. However, Microsoft had responded by changing the Web address for the site, causing the swarm of virtual arrows to miss. The main side effect was temporary frustration for some users who could not find the new site from which to download software updates.

These massive, coordinated attacks suggested that computer viruses could now be used as weapons rather than just tools for cyber vandalism. Further, anyone could be an unwitting participant. Vincent Weafer, a senior director at the computer security company Symantec, believes that "the virus-writer world and the hacker world have come together. They don't care who you are. Your machine is an asset to them."[6]

Viruses to Go

As the ways people communicate and compute change, so do the opportunities for spreading viruses and worms. Today, millions of people keep in touch using cell phones that have new features such as text messaging and the ability to send pictures. Despite their appearance of being telephones with added features, these devices are essentially tiny but fully functional computers. After all, they have a processor, memory, and data input and output devices, and they are connected using a network.

Early in 2005, McAfee, one of the leading developers of antivirus software, warned that hackers were poised to exploit more than a thousand different vulnerabilities involving mobile devices and networks. Already about fifty mobile phone viruses or other software threats have been detected. Most are Trojan horses (programs disguised to look like something harmless) or worms (such as Bropia and variants called Kelvir and Serflog). As with viruses sent by e-mail, the programs are installed when users unwittingly open infected message attachments. The programs then read the user's buddy list and send bogus instant messages (IMs) to every address they find.

Antivirus researcher Jimmy Kuo of McAfee explains what he did when his daughter asked permission to use instant messaging: "I sat her down and made her read a story about attacks before I let her log onto IM. Unfortunately, the average parent isn't going to be aware of this problem, and a person unaware of the IM threat is the biggest risk that exists for these viruses to have some success."[7]

Even experienced PC users who know how to be careful about e-mail attachments may be victimized by attachments in IMs. They may not realize that unlike ordinary text messages, IM attachments can contain executable code—and thus, viruses.

Computer security experts suggest that eventually, viruses may gain a different sort of mobility. Modern

Beware the Trojan Horse

According to the ancient Greek poet Homer, a Greek army had besieged the enemy city of Troy for ten years but could not break through its massive walls. Finally the Greeks came up with an answer. They built a huge wooden horse on wheels and left it near the city gates. One of the Greek spies convinced the Trojans it was a peace offering. The Trojans wheeled the horse into the city. While they were celebrating the peace, Greek warriors hiding inside the horse poured out, opened the gates and let in the rest of the Greek army, which quickly conquered the city.

Computer users who like to try new games or other software must beware of the modern version of the Trojan horse. Today's Trojan horses are malicious programs that masquerade as games, utilities, or other desirable software. When the user runs the program, it does something nasty such as erase data from the hard drive or launch a virus.

Users can guard against Trojan horses by downloading software only from reputable Web sites or file libraries, such as those maintained by well-known computer magazines or reputable Internet service providers.

cars are packed full of computerized systems that help control acceleration and steering, monitor fuel consumption, and provide navigation and emergency help. By 2005 online rumors were reporting possible viruses that could infect the computer systems of Lexus cars and SUVs through Bluetooth (a type of wireless network).

Toyota Motors, the manufacturer of Lexus cars, was concerned enough to investigate, although it found that the rumors of such viruses were false. Still, experts suggest that viruses could indeed be introduced into car computers. For example, hackers driving by might use their laptop or palmtop computers to beam signals with virus code into the car's wiring or Global Positioning System antennas.

Some computer visionaries, such as the late Michael Dertouzos at MIT, have predicted a time when almost every significant object in peoples' lives has computer capabilities and is part of a network.

"I'd like to hook you up to my laptop and let my
anti-virus software have a crack at you."

While having "smart homes" with appliances that
can communicate with each other is still in the future, experts warn that once these new capabilities
become reality, they will open new vulnerabilities
to be exploited by hackers or other ill-intentioned
individuals.

Computer Epidemiology

As computer networks and the programs that use
them grow ever more complex, they begin to resemble the behavior of biological organisms. Thus, people who fight outbreaks of computer viruses and
worms see their jobs as more and more resembling
those of epidemiologists, doctors who study how
diseases spread in humans and other living organisms. They not only study the disease organisms
themselves, but also the vectors, or carriers, that al-

low the infection to spread. Epidemiologists also have to look at how different populations or groups of people might be more susceptible or more resistant to a given disease. Finally, they also have to consider how a disease organism may evolve, gaining new capabilities that might make it more deadly or harder to stop.

There are many parallels between the fight against biological disease and the fight against digital disease represented by computer viruses and worms. Just as their medical counterparts study an organism's genetic makeup, computer epidemiologists analyze a virus's code in order to understand its capabilities. While doing so, some of the questions they ask include: What vulnerabilities does it seek to exploit? When a computer is infected, what happens? How fast is the virus likely to spread, and what might be its overall impact on the network?

Like medical researchers, computer virus researchers now often look at past infections in order to understand what future ones might be like. They

Sneaky Spyware

Many computer users may discover that they have been victimized by another sort of Trojan horse program called spyware. Typically the user downloads and installs a desirable program, such as for music file sharing. However, while the program is being installed, other programs are also secretly being put in place. Some programs are just adware that merely downloads and displays ads. Others are true spyware, which can secretly track and transmit information about the user's Web activities or, worse, capture passwords or account numbers.

Sometimes the user is not told at all that spyware will be installed. In other cases it is mentioned only in user agreements full of legalese that hardly anyone takes the time to read. Users may suspect they have a spyware-infested machine when normal activities start slowing down or strange windows open during Web-surfing sessions.

try to anticipate those future attacks and decide how they will attempt to deal with them.

Epidemiologists who focus only on the behavior of the disease organism may not sufficiently take account of human behavior, which can be critical for understanding many diseases. Similarly, since so many computer infections rely on the unwitting cooperation of users, an understanding of users' psychology is important.

However, one significant difference between biological viruses and computer viruses is that the living viruses do not really have motives or purposes. Computer viruses are (thus far, anyway) all created by human beings who do have motives for their actions. And what motivates the creator of viruses and worms is a matter of considerable interest to the computer community.

Chapter 4

Why Do They Do It?

There are many reasons people create computer viruses and other potentially destructive programs. Understanding the possible motives and goals of creators of malicious software, or malware, can help both security professionals and ordinary users determine which risks are the most serious. In looking at virus creators, it is important to realize that their level of experience, their capabilities, and their likely motives all help determine the seriousness of the threat they pose.

Script Kiddies

Sometimes, a virus is the creation of a youngster who does not intend to harm anyone in particular. There are many reasons why a bright, technically minded teenager might start fooling around with computer viruses. The motive might be mainly curiosity—learning how viruses work and then trying to create a virus of one's own. There can also be the desire to rebel or somehow get back at the adult world represented by big corporations or government computer systems. Finally, there is the drive to compare oneself with one's peers and gain bragging rights by successfully attacking a Web site.

"Mommy -- Jimmy just wrote his first computer virus!"

Within the world of computer virus creators, the experienced programmers who write viruses from scratch look down on "script kiddies." This is their term for usually young, would-be hackers who do not know enough about programming to create original viruses or worms. What these novices do is download a so-called virus kit that consists of options for pieces of executable code that can be linked together to form a functioning virus. These virus kits are generally available on the same sort of underground Web sites that contain illicit or pirated software and other dubious files.

Fortunately for the computing community, because they are so similar to known viruses, those created by script kiddies can usually be easily recognized and neutralized by antivirus programs. Still, the damage they do can be substantial, and when caught, the perpetrator can be in a great deal of trouble. For example, in August 2003 nineteen-year-old Jeffrey Lee Parson created a simple variant of the destructive Blaster worm that had clogged more than 9 million computers earlier that year. After his worm, designated "Blaster.B" by experts, had infected about fifty thousand machines, Parson was caught. He later received an eighteen-month prison sentence and agreed to perform 225 hours of community service.

In 2005 Jeffrey Lee Parson was sentenced to eighteen months in prison for modifying the Blaster Internet worm so that it would attack the Microsoft Web site.

Jeff Hall, a topflight computer security expert, said he was not very impressed by Parson or by the arrest: "Big deal. It's nice they caught somebody, but . . . at the end of the day, it's a 19-year old kid who took some code off the Internet, tweaked it a bit and tossed it back out there. He's not a genius."[8]

However, some people in the computing industry believe that this and other prosecutions for relatively minor computer crimes are a way to signal that such activities will no longer be tolerated in this increasingly security-conscious society.

Troubling (and Troubled) Young Hackers

Some knowledgeable observers consider the prosecution of such amateur virus writers an overreaction driven by fear and anxiety about a little-understood technology. As technology writers Katie Hafner and John Markoff noted back in the mid-1990s:

> For many in this country, hackers have become the new magicians: they have mastered the machines that control modern life. This is a time of transition when young people are comfortable with a new technology that intimidates their elders. It's not surprising that parents, federal investigators, prosecutors and judges often panic when confronted with something they believe is too complicated to understand.[9]

It is true that the motives of hackers who have substantial skills are often more complex and ambiguous than those of script kiddies. Some of these talented individuals, who come from a culture that focuses on curiosity and a sense of exploration and play, do not necessarily set out to damage computer systems or steal property. They just want to see what happens next. For example, Spooky, a seventeen-year-old who founded the Codebreakers virus-writing crew, told an interviewer, "I love to write such code . . . to see them survive in the wild is kind of nice also!"[10]

On the other hand, many virus writers seem to be part of an alienated subculture—bright but bitter and often violent in their imagery and expressions.

Why Do They Pick on Windows?

There is a good reason why most virus creators focus on computers running Microsoft Windows, rather than writing viruses for Macintosh or Linux systems. A virus is a program, and a program has to be compiled into instructions for a particular computer processor and operating system. For example, a program written for a Macintosh will not be recognized by a computer running Windows.

Since more than 90 percent of personal computers run Windows, it simply makes sense for a person who wants to spread a virus to design it for Windows machines. So, although there are viruses written for Macintosh, Linux, and other systems, the vast majority of viruses target Windows.

Windows also has some special features that make it attractive to virus writers. Many Windows programs can run macros or scripts, which are like miniprograms that control the software's behavior. There is also a facility called ActiveX that allows programs to be run from Web sites in the user's browser. These functions make it easy to add new features to software and to accommodate new file formats. Unfortunately, anything that can run a program can potentially harbor a virus, and these facilities have been exploited by numerous viruses in recent years.

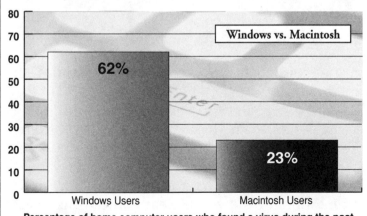

Percentage of home computer users who found a virus during the past two years.

Source: ConsumerReports.org, 2002.

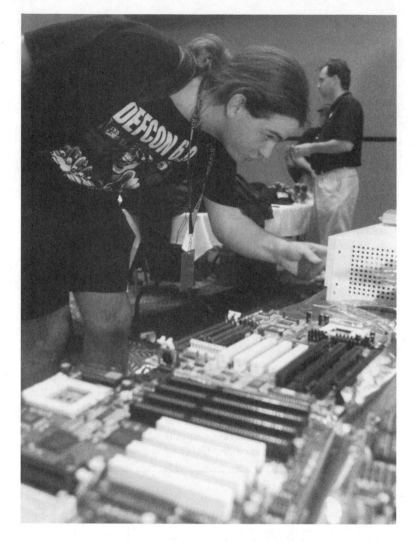

The popularity of computer hacking has led to hacking conventions, such as this one in 1999, where hackers can examine the latest hacking-related hardware and software.

Internet columnist Jon Katz writes about online culture and reports:

> I get e-mail from these young men every day. There is a hostile streak in this new universe, whose mailing lists and chat rooms are filled with "flames," insults and virulent confrontation. Some of the e-mail that comes in is riveting; some is fairly savage. It's a rare day somebody doesn't urge me to die. When I respond, my correspondents are often surprised and

apologetic. They didn't, they tell me, think I would really read their message.[11]

Unfortunately for the inhabitants of the more virulent chat rooms, in the environment created by the terrorist attacks of September 11, 2001, threats (including threats of computer attack) that once might have been dismissed as mere bluster or playacting can have real consequences. The results can include a visit from agents of the FBI. Such a serious consequence can await even those whose motives are altruistic, hackers known as white hats.

Shades of Gray

Hackers sometimes use the term *white hat* to describe those among them whose skills are devoted to exploration or to helping users better protect their systems. A white hat might, for example, find a system that has a hidden vulnerability and send an e-mail to the system administrator suggesting that he or she download and install a software patch. White hats may technically break the law in entering systems without permission, but their motives are not those of criminals. Sometimes, in fact, white hats can also work for security companies or help emergency response teams identify and counteract new viruses and worms. White hats are also sometimes called ethical hackers.

Black hats, on the other hand, as the name suggests, are less benign in their motives. While some simply enjoy creating viruses that are hard to stop and get some satisfaction from gaining notoriety, many of them are motivated by money. They may employ viruses to take over machines and use them to send bulk e-mail (spam) that seeks to trick users into revealing credit card or other information. Others attempt to extort money from a company by threatening a computer attack. This is a relatively rare occurrence, however, because the risk of getting caught is high.

Often, however, a hacker's motives are not so clear-cut. A young hacker who created a hacking group called Genocide2600 points this out in the group's manifesto:

> People generally believe that hackers have malicious intent. . . . I do admit that "YES" there are those that are out to destroy . . . but for the most part we are in the pursuit of knowledge. I do not

Hacking Hollywood

Starting with *War Games* in 1983, Hollywood films began to paint a lurid picture of young hackers whose skills threatened dire consequences, perhaps even the destruction of the world. Meanwhile, some hackers seemed to enjoy their newfound celebrity status, while others reacted with disdain or even outrage.

The 1995 movie *Hackers* in particular was strongly criticized by much of the hacker community. They argued that the movie lacked accuracy, which was admittedly not unusual in Hollywood's treatment of technical matters. But they also resented what they saw as the movie's portrayal of hackers as awkward teenage nerds who lacked real understanding of the technology. In response, a number of promotional Web pages for the movie were broken into and modified by hackers.

Actors Angelina Jolie and Johnny Lee Miller appear in a scene from the 1995 film Hackers.

claim to be a 100% law abiding person, nor does
the group. . . . People for all time have feared
what they do not understand, what they do not
know. You don't know us; you don't understand
us. OK. Sure. Whatever. Go ahead take the criminals and terrorists away that fight for your rights.
After you have lost the battle because your sol-
diers are gone at your own hand, you'll have no
one to blame but yourself. We fight with the
greatest tools of all, our intellect and courage.[12]

The wide-ranging arguments offered by this
hacker convey the conflicting attitudes of many of
his colleagues. Many hackers do seek knowledge and
try to minimize the destructive effects of their actions. The individuals whose writings appear in the
hacker magazine *2600*, for example, include many
who see hacking as a way to defend civil liberties
from a heavy-handed government and to keep information technology from being controlled by what
they claim are greedy corporations.

At the same time, hackers may be tempted by
greed or anger or even idealism to push the envelope
and do something that might have far-reaching consequences. Sometimes hackers with such conflicting,
complex motives are called gray hats.

Viruses, Spamming, and Phishing

A troubling recent development is the close cooperation between hackers and organized groups of criminals. This can be seen most commonly in the connection of viruses to spam, the unwanted messages
that crowd so many electronic mailboxes today. Greg
Mastoras of Sophos, an antivirus research company,
notes: "Unfortunately in 2004, we saw increased col-
laboration among cybercriminals through organized
crime rings and collusion between virus writers and
spammers. . . . We also saw financial motivation become the driving force between spam and viruses."[13]

An entire underground economy has developed around the spam industry. A typical scenario might go like this: A spam mailing service hires a virus writer. The virus writer creates a virus that takes over thousands of users' PCs, usually without their knowledge and without affecting the everyday operation of the machines. The virus installs a spambot program on each computer that receives spam messages and then addresses and does the mailing using the facilities on the infested system. The spam service then sells access to the spambots to a spammer, who pays to get his or her message out to millions of users.

Most spam tends to carry the same sorts of messages with minor variations: sexual or pornographic offers, low-cost medications or software, counterfeits of expensive, name-brand merchandise like Rolex watches, and so on. Spam imposes costs in time and resources on the providers of e-mail services, as well as annoys users. People can also waste money on ineffective or even potentially dangerous products they buy from spammers.

However, starting in 2003 a much more nefarious use of spam emerged in the form of a technique called phishing. Phishing e-mails pretend to be from legitimate institutions such as banks or popular sites. The message typically warns the user that his or her account information needs to be validated, perhaps as part of a routine security procedure.

The user is asked to click on a Web link in the message. After doing so, the user sees what seems to be the normal Web site of the bank or other company. However the site actually belongs to the criminals who sent the message. When the user enters passwords, credit card numbers, or account numbers into the form on the Web page, the criminals can use the information to charge merchandise, withdraw money, or even create new credit accounts in the hapless user's name—a crime called identity theft.

Without the latest security software, computer users run the risk of having personal information, such as a credit card number, stolen by hackers.

Another technique uses deceptive e-mail to trick users into installing a hidden keylogging program, which waits until the user visits a legitimate banking site. The program then records the user's account name, password, and other information and transmits it to the criminals.

Clearly, viruses and other harmful software can be used for a wide variety of purposes, ranging from the curious and careless to the criminal. And just as it is hard to get a handle on the complex motives behind virus-related activities, so, too, is it hard to measure the economic and social impact of computer viruses.

Chapter 5

Counting
the Cost

At a time when the public is concerned about threats as diverse as energy shortages, global warming, and even bioterrorism, it is necessary to place the threat of computer viruses in context. Experts are divided on the seriousness of the problem, with some stressing the possibility of devastating attacks by cyber terrorists while others believe the threat has been exaggerated.

One way to approach this question is to try to determine how much computer viruses and other attacks are costing society. But even this task is difficult. To begin with, even experts cannot always agree on how to measure cost. Complicating the picture, computer viruses potentially have several different impacts.

The direct financial costs to organizations victimized by virus attacks include the expense involved in finding and eradicating the viruses and possibly restoring lost data, usually from backup files. To this can be added the costs of buying and installing antivirus software, firewalls, and other virus prevention tools, as well as training system administrators and users.

Businesses may also face costly indirect effects from an attack. If a company's Web site is forced offline, customers may not be able to buy its products or services. Even after the site is restored, some customers may be reluctant to patronize the business because they are afraid hackers might be able to steal their personal information.

Finally, computer crimes such as online fraud, identity theft, and phishing are estimated to cost consumers billions of dollars a year. To the extent these crimes can be aided by the use of viruses (such as to send spam or plant Trojan horse programs), some part of this cost could also be credited to viruses.

There have been some attempts to estimate the costs of particular virus or worm outbreaks. The research firm Computer Economics reported that dur-

Economic Impact of Major Virus Attacks, 1999–2003		
Year	Virus Name	Worldwide Financial Impact (in U.S. Dollars)
2003	Nachi	$500 Million
2003	Blaster	$400 Million
2003	Slammer	$1.25 Billion
2002	Badtrands	$400 Million
2002	BugBear	$500 Million
2002	Klez	$750 Million
2001	Nimda	$635 Million
2001	Code Red	$2.62 Billion
2001	SirCam	$1.15 Billion
2000	Love Bug	$8.75 Billion
1999	Melissa	$1.10 Billion
1999	Explorer	$1.10 Billion

Source: Computer Economics.

ing 2001, a banner year for worms and viruses, the total cost caused by some of the major culprits included $635 million for the Nimda worm, $2.62 billion for the Code Red worm, $1.15 billion for the Sir-Cam virus, and a whopping $8.75 billion for the Love Bug virus.

In all, Computer Economics estimated that the total economic impact of viruses was $13.2 billion in 2001. Some observers believe these estimates may be too high, and the criteria used to arrive at them have not been revealed to the public. Certain costs might be attributed directly to a specific virus, or they may be part of a general response designed to tighten computer security. Because of these problems, in recent years, companies have become more reluctant to try to estimate the economic impact of viruses. Still, a consensus of experts' estimates suggests that the annual cost of dealing with virus damage and trying to prevent future attacks is in the billions of dollars.

The Prevalence of Attacks

Cost is only one aspect of the impact of computer viruses. People also judge the impact of an attack by how widespread its effects are. A number of surveys can offer some data about the impact of computer viruses (and other aspects of computer crime) on society. The FBI and the Computer Security Institute (CSI) conduct an annual survey of computer security incidents and practices. For 2004, about 53 percent of respondents reported unauthorized access to their computers during the past year. This is down from a high of 70 percent in 2000.

About three-quarters of reported attacks involved viruses. As for the source of attacks, businesses reported that security incidents were divided about evenly between those coming from inside the company and attacks from outside. The prevalence of attacks suggests that anyone who uses computers at

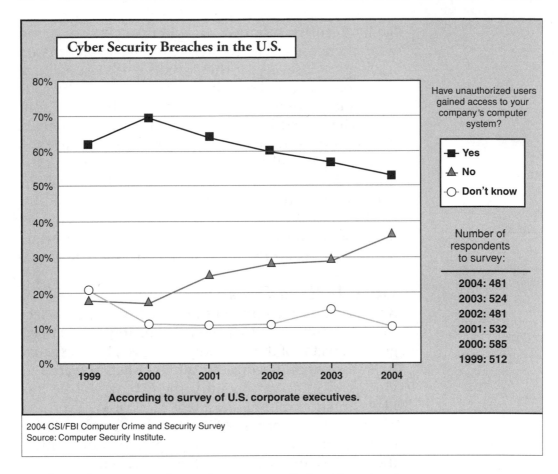

Cyber Security Breaches in the U.S.

Have unauthorized users gained access to your company's computer system?

- ■ Yes
- ▲ No
- ○ Don't know

Number of respondents to survey:

2004: 481
2003: 524
2002: 481
2001: 532
2000: 585
1999: 512

According to survey of U.S. corporate executives.

2004 CSI/FBI Computer Crime and Security Survey
Source: Computer Security Institute.

work or home needs to be aware of the threat of viruses, worms, and related forms of attack and to take positive measures to minimize the risk.

Viruses and Other Computer Crimes

Several costs associated with computer attacks are not caused directly by viruses, but viruses are often important tools used by the attackers. Denial-of-service attacks, in which access to Web sites is blocked, caused an estimated $26 million in damage to those who responded to the FBI/CSI survey. Many attacks are launched from computers that have been infected with viruses or worms.

An even more costly activity is identity theft, a crime in which information such as credit card or

Social Security numbers are obtained by criminals who then use them to steal cash from victims or make purchases using their credit cards. According to a report by the research firm Synovate for the Federal Trade Commission, about 10 million people were victimized by some form of identity theft in 2003—and more recent statistics show the rate for this crime is still increasing. The same report estimated the total cost to society at $50 billion. While about two-thirds of the financial costs were paid by banks and other businesses, the individual victims faced hours of frustrating calls and letters as they attempted to repair the damage done to their credit.

Other Indirect Costs

Americans have embraced the online world, and electronic commerce has become probably the fastest growing sector of the economy. However, business analysts worry that if people are afraid of falling victim to viruses, swindles, or identity theft, they will be less likely to shop online. President George W. Bush expressed this concern in 2004 when he signed a bill increasing prison sentences for perpetrators of identity theft: "The crime of identity theft undermines the basic trust on which our economy depends. Identity theft harms not only its direct victims, but also many businesses and customers whose confidence is shaken."[14]

A 2004 survey by RSA Security suggests that many consumers are becoming reluctant to entrust their personal information even with established banks and other institutions. Sixty-three percent of respondents said they were more informed about identity theft than they had been in 2003, but only 18 percent felt more safe, while 26 percent considered themselves to be more vulnerable. It is likely that continuing stories about viruses, computer break-ins, and online scams are contributing to this unease. It is very difficult, however, to attach a price tag to the loss of business a company might have had.

The Cost of Defense

The cost of maintaining virus research teams and developing and using antivirus software and related tools is somewhat easier to quantify. In 2003 an industry analysis published by *InfoWorld* estimated that the market for antivirus products amounted to $2.6 billion in 2003 and was expected to reach $9.4 billion by 2009.

Of course, this is just the cost for the products themselves. In the corporate world, employees have to be trained in the use of the software. Further, fighting viruses is only part of the overall problem of computer security, which also includes the efforts

2004: A Virus Snapshot

New viruses with new capabilities are constantly emerging. In its 2004 report, the antivirus company Sophos reported 10,724 new viruses, 50 percent more than the previous year. They reported the total of known viruses as 97,536, though the existence of many minor variations makes counts rather unreliable. Here are the top 10 viruses of 2004 in terms of the percentage of infections reported:

W32/Netsky-P	22.6%
W32/Zafi-B	18.8%
W32/Sasser	14.2%
W32/Netsky-B	7.4%
W32/Netsky-D	6.1%
W32/Netsky-Z	3.7%
W32/MyDoom-A	2.4%
W32/Sober-I	1.9%
W32/Netsky-C	1.8%
W32/Bagle-AA	1.6%
Others	19.5%

As shown above, variants of the Netsky virus accounted for more than 40 percent of the reported viruses. And as indicated by W32 (Windows 32) prefix, all of the top viruses were written for Windows systems.

This computer screen displays the Hoaxbusters Web page, which debunks false warnings about nonexistent worms and viruses.

to keep hackers, industrial spies, or other unauthorized users from breaking into systems and stealing information. Tightening overall security in turn reduces the risk that someone will be able to introduce a virus into a system. The costs for computer security as a whole now run into tens of billions of dollars.

Hoaxes and Hyperbole

Clearly, both the effects of viruses and the efforts to fight them can be expensive. But sometimes the virus is not even there, and any effort to fight it is

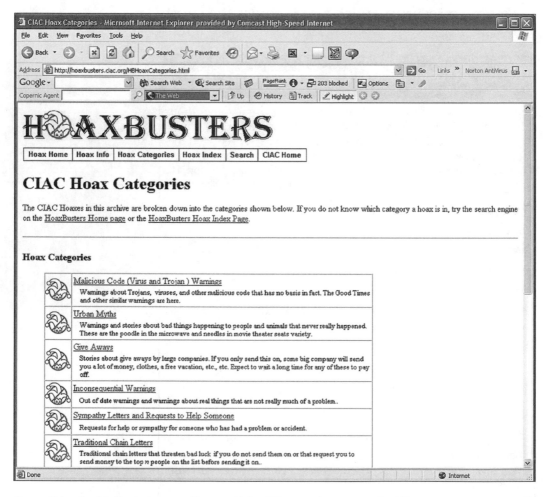

Source: University of California, Lawrence Livermore National Library, and the Department of Energy.

therefore wasted. In today's media-saturated world, emerging problems tend to get blown out of proportion. When this is combined with millions of relatively inexperienced users joining the online world each year, the result is a fertile ground for hoaxes of all kinds. One common form is an e-mail giving a false warning about some new virus.

The Web site Vmyths.com debunks virus hoaxes. Its writers argue that virus hysteria is often promoted by three groups:

> Gullible users—many of them new to computers, some of them not-so-new—fall for virus hoaxes and believe virus myths every day. . . .

> Antivirus firms and the media propel [a type of hysteria] which comes as a dire warning about a "horrifying new virus" capable of destroying the Internet. A global panic ensues and can last for months, followed by an amazing anti-climax. . . .

> Gullible users alone propel a second type of [hysteria] which starts either as a hoax or as an urban legend. Again, a global panic ensues and can last for months.[15]

Admittedly, it is often hard to know what level of urgency is appropriate in responding to a virus. *Computerworld* editor Maryfran Johnson notes that security companies often agonize over how much alarm to raise when [virus] outbreaks first occur. In the frantic guessing game in the early hours of a virus's appearance, some prefer to hype rather than understate the dangers."[16]

Sometimes, too, the supposed virus attack turns out to be a hoax. A classic example of a virus hoax was the (nonexistent) Good Times Virus that plagued the Internet through most of the late 1990s. According to the e-mail that spread the hoax:

What makes this virus so terrifying . . . is the fact that no program needs to be exchanged for a new computer to be infected. It can be spread through the existing e-mail systems of the InterNet. Once a computer is infected, one of several things can happen. If the computer contains a hard drive, that will most likely be destroyed. If the program is not stopped, the computer's processor will be placed in an nth-complexity infinite binary loop—which can severely damage the processor if left running that way too long. Unfortunately, most novice computer users will not realize what is happening until it is far too late.[17]

The Good Times message was fairly typical of hoaxes. It made extravagant claims about the potency of the virus and its destructive potential. Further, it used technical-sounding nonsense such as "an nth-complexity infinite binary loop" in claiming that it could damage the actual computer hardware.

While many virus hoaxes simply waste time and cause unnecessary anxiety, a number of actual worms or viruses (including the recent Sober worm) are actually spread by e-mails that describe a nonexistent virus. They provide an attachment that they claim will cure the infection. The attachment, however, actually contains a virus.

It is difficult to determine the cost of virus hoaxes. At the least, they divert attention from fighting real viruses, can result in the loss of work time, and may lead users to ignore real virus threats later.

Future Threats

While keeping current virus threats in perspective, it is also necessary to look at what some experts suggest are some emerging or possible uses of viruses as weapons, either in a military conflict or by terrorists.

The actual use of computer viruses or related tactics by the U.S. military against an enemy has never been confirmed. However, a 2005 hearing by the U.S. Senate's Armed Services Committee revealed the existence of a military unit of the U.S. Strategic Command (Stratcom) devoted to defending against attacks on the nation's vital networks, including power, telephone, and computer services, as well as developing weapons to be used in such attacks on future enemies. Some observers believe that predecessors of this group may have already tried out their tactics in the war between NATO and Serbia in the late 1990s, as well as in Afghanistan in 2002 and Iraq in 2003. However, the secrecy surrounding all such special operations makes it impossible to know their extent.

Experts suggest, however, that in future wars it is likely that trained "information warriors" (as well as some hackers) will try to shut down Web sites in the enemy country or possibly deface them or use them to post their own propaganda. Viruses are a logical weapon to use to launch Web-based attacks and to cause business disruption and economic losses. Thus, it is quite possible that viruses and hacker attacks will play a part in the wars of the twenty-first century.

Payback in the Workplace

Surveys have shown that most destructive computer attacks on businesses come from disgruntled employees, not outside hackers. In part, this is because insiders are more likely to know the features and vulnerabilities of a company's computer system.

One type of program used in some insider attacks is the logic bomb. This is a program that is designed to do something destructive (such as erase a company's payroll data) when a given condition occurs. For example, an employee who anticipates being fired may set such a program to be triggered a certain number of days after his or her termination. To prevent this sort of attack, it is now a common policy to secure an employee's computer even before he or she is fired or laid off. The employee is then escorted out of the building.

Cyber Terrorism?

For many people, the ultimate threat from computer viruses is that terrorists might use them to bring down vital systems such as the power grid, air traffic control, or communication systems the U.S. relies on.

Following the terrorist attacks of September 11, 2001, experts and the general public alike became concerned about the vulnerability of the basic systems or infrastructure that ties the national economy and society together. How likely, and how serious, a terrorist attack using computer viruses might be remains a matter of speculation. However, in recent years hackers who call themselves hacktivists have penetrated various government and corporate Web sites and added their own messages—roughly the electronic equivalent of graffiti. These actions are intended to make a political point while causing little real damage.

In fact, there have been reports of hacker groups in China, Pakistan, and other countries responding to American actions (such as the accidental bombing of the Chinese embassy in Sarajevo during the war against Serbia) by attacking various U.S. Web sites. Homeland security experts believe that al Qaeda or other international terrorist groups are growing more sophisticated in their computer knowledge and may try to use viruses or denial-of-service attacks against economic targets such as banks or online stores.

Given the growing importance of online commerce to the overall economy of the United States and other developed nations, such economic terrorism may be an appealing and relatively low-risk tactic for terrorist groups. The CIA seemed to confirm this threat by conducting an extensive war game in May 2005 in which a hypothetical alliance of anti-American organizations launched simulated attacks that were expected to have devastating results.

On the other hand, many experts feel that the type of cyber terrorism most feared by the general public

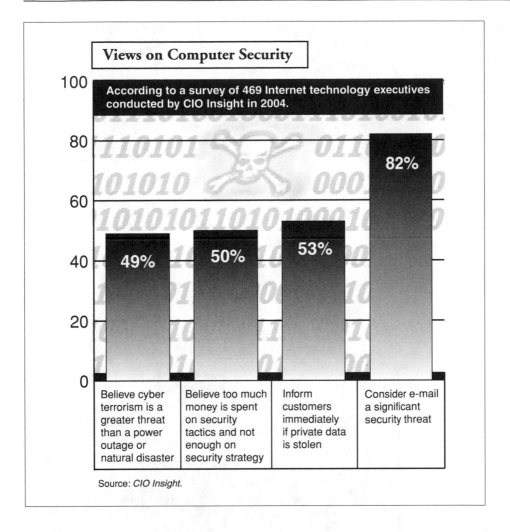

Views on Computer Security

According to a survey of 469 Internet technology executives conducted by CIO Insight in 2004.

Believe cyber terrorism is a greater threat than a power outage or natural disaster	Believe too much money is spent on security tactics and not enough on security strategy	Inform customers immediately if private data is stolen	Consider e-mail a significant security threat
49%	50%	53%	82%

Source: *CIO Insight.*

is relatively unlikely. Sensitive facilities such as power plants or air traffic control systems are generally isolated from the global Internet or use their own secure networks. However, careless workers might create insecure connections that could be used by hackers to access control systems directly or to introduce viruses that might cripple the systems. (Wireless links are particularly vulnerable because unless users make use of security procedures they can be accessed by anyone driving by with a laptop computer.)

Facilities such as chemical plants generally have multiple physical safety systems that might prevent

Some experts are concerned that an attack on the computer network of sensitive facilities such as this chemical storage site could endanger the public.

a hacker's command from causing a spill or other disaster, but this assumes the safety systems themselves are functional, reliable, and regularly tested. Since September 11, 2001, both electronic and physical security at such facilities have been upgraded to varying extents.

In congressional testimony in early 2005, FBI director Robert Mueller suggested that terrorist groups may be recruiting computer experts, but he also said that "most hackers do not have the resources or motivation to attack U.S. critical information infrastructures."[18] Since these capabilities may change, continuing attention to potential threats is needed.

The considerable media attention to cyber terrorism in recent years has also brought responses that seek to put the threat in perspective. For example, a 2002 report by the Center for Strategic and International Studies, a prominent think tank, points out that much of the nation's infrastructure (such as water systems) is decentralized so that thousands of separate systems limit the damage that could be done by any one attack. Power and communications systems also have considerable redundancy, as can be seen in how they deal with routine failures. The report's author concludes by saying, "The sky is not falling, and cyber weapons seem to be of limited value in attacking national power or intimidating citizens."[19]

All in all, the risks and potential costs of computer viruses and other forms of computer attack can be considerable, but they are hard to assess. Often there seem to be new vulnerabilities being highlighted every day. However, the news from the front lines of the war against these digital invaders is not all bad. Experts have created tools and techniques to identify and stop virus attacks, and these techniques are constantly being upgraded.

Chapter 6

Fighting Back

Many computer viruses and worms evidence considerable ingenuity on the part of their creators. However, for every bright person who is tempted to try to find a new way to infect computer systems, there is probably another bright person who finds challenge and excitement in unmasking and eliminating the intruders. As a result of the efforts of talented virus fighters, a number of tools and strategies are available to help users protect their systems.

Antivirus Software

Many computer users have access to programs that can intercept viruses or eradicate existing infections —antivirus programs such as those sold by McAfee or Symantec. Many new computers purchased today come with introductory or trial versions of antivirus software, and the use of such software is now simple and routine enough to be considered an essential part of safe computing.

Tech TV reporter Becky Worley describes the operation of antivirus programs using a familiar scenario: "Think of an AV [antivirus] program as an x-ray machine at the airport. Each file scanned as it enters your computer is like a carry-on bag. The AV program scans

the file looking for known malicious files, just as a screener tries to identify explosives and weapons."[20]

No matter who produces them, antivirus programs use the same basic approach, a constantly updated dictionary containing bits of code from all identified viruses. The antivirus program scans files on the hard drive, other media, or from incoming e-mail attachments. If it finds a sequence of bits that matches the signature for a virus, the file is flagged as infected. At that point the user might be offered the option of deleting the file, placing it in a special quarantine area where it cannot be executed, or in some cases, repairing the file by removing the viral code and replacing it with the correct data. (This last option is typically used for files that are needed by the operating system of a computer already infected by a virus.)

Trial versions of antivirus software come preinstalled on many personal computers sold today.

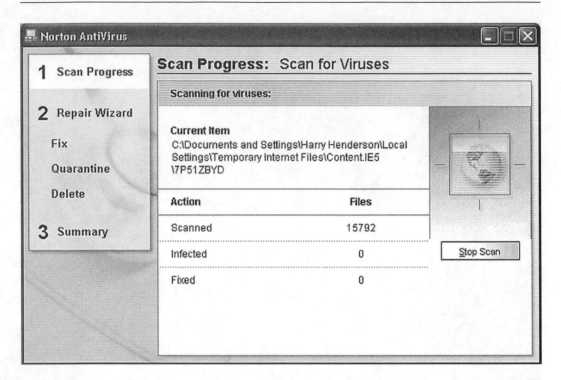

This computer screen displays the results of a scan by Norton AntiVirus, one of several popular virus protection programs.

The dictionary approach is effective for detecting and dealing with known viruses. It does require that the dictionary be updated regularly (at least weekly) in order to identify the new viruses that are constantly appearing. Most programs now include an option to have the updated dictionary regularly downloaded automatically.

Cop on the Beat

Virus lists are not perfect, however. They are much less effective with polymorphic viruses that can change their code as they reproduce (or conceal it through encryption), making them harder to identify. The dictionary approach is then like a guard at a gate checking people's papers to see if they are on a list of people with criminal records. If someone with mischief in mind uses a different identity, the guard may let them through.

For this reason, modern antivirus programs have a second layer of defense. They also watch for suspicious behavior. Just as a guard in a store will take action if a shopper starts stuffing an expensive pair of designer jeans into a bag, the antivirus program can look for software that is attempting to do something out of the ordinary. To do this, it monitors the calls or requests that programs make to the computer's operating system. For example, if some program attempts to copy data into an executable program file rather than a document, the antivirus program will halt the activity and alert the computer's user.

This approach can halt viruses that would get past a dictionary check, but it has the drawback of often flagging legitimate actions. For example, many programs do store certain types of information in executable files. As a result, the user may be bombarded by cryptic messages while running a piece of legitimate software obtained from a reliable source. Users are faced with an unpleasant choice: Either click No and possibly halt legitimate activities or click Yes and possibly allow an incoming virus or other malicious program to carry out its attack.

Layers of Defense

Some antivirus programs have additional strategies for dealing with viruses. One approach is to create a "sandbox"—a sort of simulated computer within the real computer's memory in which the suspect code is allowed to run. If the code shows signs of destructive or suspicious behavior (such as encrypting itself), it is then prevented from executing on the real computer.

Virus protection (and computer security in general) also takes a "defense in depth" approach. Many antivirus programs combine several of the strategies for identifying and coping with viruses. And antivirus programs are only one part of a recommended security system for today's computers. Security experts believe that defense against viruses begins on the network, before attacks even reach the PC itself.

Plugging the Gaps

In order for computers to connect to each other and the Internet, there have to be protocols—that is, agreements about how data is to be organized into packets and routed for various applications and purposes. The connections that a computer makes available to Internet traffic are called ports. Each port has certain designated purposes, such as e-mail, http (Web), and so on.

The problem is that networks were designed using the assumption that programs will generally be well behaved and negotiate properly for access to services on other computers. However, operating systems and software often have vulnerabilities that may allow intruders to gain access to a computer. A worm or virus can take advantage of such vulnerabilities to force its way onto the computer.

For example, one common type of vulnerability is called a buffer overflow. A buffer is an area of memory that a program uses to store incoming information such as an address. Unfortunately, some programs accept strings of data that extend beyond the buffer into other parts of the memory being used by the program—for example, an area for holding executable commands. This means that an intruder who gains access to a port running the vulnerable program can feed it code that might install a virus or Trojan horse program on the user's hard drive.

One defense against this type of attack is for operating-system and software developers to be alert for new vulnerabilities and to send users updated patches to address newly discovered problems. Those who study viruses say that because new vulnerabilities are being discovered each week, it is important for users to update their systems regularly. The problem is that many users either forget or simply neglect to download the updates. Increasingly, however, the updates can be performed without any action on the user's part. Features such as Microsoft

Windows Update allow patches to be downloaded and installed automatically from a trusted Web site.

Operating systems such as Microsoft Windows and major applications such as Microsoft Office also receive major updates from time to time. (These are often called service packs.) Although it takes some time, these should generally be installed unless there is a good reason not to, such as a hardware incompatibility.

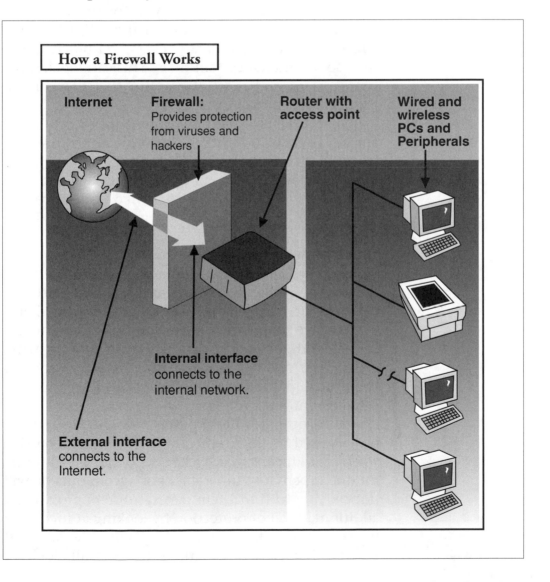

How a Firewall Works

Internet

Firewall: Provides protection from viruses and hackers

Router with access point

Wired and wireless PCs and Peripherals

Internal interface connects to the internal network.

External interface connects to the Internet.

Guarding the Gates

While patches can fix known vulnerabilities, there is another form of defense that can block intruders before they even get access to the computer or network. This is the firewall, so-named because, like the protective layer that prevents an overheated automobile engine from setting fire to a fuel tank, this defense puts a protective layer between incoming viruses and the PC or local network.

There are actually several types of firewalls. The lowest level is the network layer firewall, which examines the details of data packets and blocks those that do not match certain rules. This can block some types of viruses that are attempting to achieve unauthorized access to the PC.

A higher level, called an application firewall, examines packets in terms of the applications they are being sent to (such as Web browsers or e-mail). The firewall recognizes what an e-mail message or a Web page http request should look like, and it rejects packets that are improperly formatted.

Routers and Personal Firewalls

Firewalls are now available in a form that is inexpensive and convenient for home users. Often, all that is needed is an inexpensive router. The router is a hardware device that connects the computers in a household together (either with Ethernet cable or wirelessly) and also connects to the device, such as a cable or digital subscriber line (DSL) modem, that provides Internet access.

Among other features, routers hide the network addresses used by the local computers from the outside world. This means that hackers who may be scanning for open (perhaps vulnerable) ports from outside will not be able to find them. Many routers provide an additional level of protection by looking at incoming packets. If a packet contains inappropriate data that may be characteristic of viruses, the firewall blocks it.

Ten Steps for Virus-Free Computing

All computer users can greatly reduce their chance of becoming victims of viruses or other computer attacks by following these basic steps. The goal is to put multiple barriers between one's system and potential attackers while not becoming overly paranoid.

1. Install antivirus software. Keep the subscription up-to-date and set the program to download updated virus-detection files regularly.

2. Make sure the antivirus program is set to scan incoming files automatically, including e-mail attachments.

3. Use a software firewall—either the one that comes with Windows, another operating system, or a third-party product. This is particularly important for users with high-speed Internet access. For added protection, connect a hardware router between the PC and the DSL or cable modem.

4. Set the system's Internet security settings as high as possible, unless a lower setting is necessary for an application to work.

5. Only open e-mail attachments that are from a known source. Do not click on Web links in e-mail messages, even if the sender appears to be a familiar company such as a bank, eBay, or PayPal.

6. Treat attachments in instant messages or chat messages with the same caution as with e-mail.

7. Be very careful with files received through file-sharing services. Download software only from known reputable sites.

8. Install and run an antispyware program.

9. Be cautious about e-mail containing warnings about viruses. It is likely a hoax and may even contain a virus itself. Check a site such as Hoaxbusters (www.hoaxbusters.com) for more information.

10. Help educate family members, friends, and coworkers about good computer security practices.

Although a router with its built-in firewall feature offers solid basic protection against intruders, users can also obtain an additional software firewall. These programs can perform further inspections and often provide more detailed reports about attempted attacks. However, users will have to tell the software

about programs that should be allowed to go
through, and the reports the software generates may
include technical information that many users will
not know how to interpret. Nevertheless, Microsoft
recommends that Windows users allow the Windows firewall to operate or, if they prefer, replace it
with firewall software from another company.

Wireless Security

Advancing technology continues to create new vulnerabilities to hackers and creators of malicious software. For example, many laptop computers today offer the option of a wireless connection to the
Internet. A typical home setup may have a modem
connected to the Internet and to a wireless router,
which in turn connects to the computer. With such
a combination, a user can use a computer in any
room in the home and still access the Internet.

Wireless network connections are convenient, but
many users do not realize that any computers that
use an access point of this sort are actually using a
radio signal that can be intercepted. For example, it
is quite possible for a neighbor (or even someone
driving by) to pick up the signal and connect to
one's modem. Further, if the computer is set up to allow sharing of files, this means that a stranger can
make a network connection and be able to browse
one's hard drive or, going the other way, insert unwanted or malicious software onto the disk.

For users, the good news is that wireless routers
and other gear can be secured against such intrusions. The software that comes with such devices
makes it possible for users to select hard-to-guess
identifiers and passwords and to enable strong forms
of encryption.

Blocking Spam

Users can also take steps to block spam e-mail that
can be used to trick them into installing viruses or

"OUR SPAM WILL CONTACT YOUR SPAM..."

Trojan horse programs. Although spam can still be plentiful in the e-mail boxes of users, there are a number of ways to reduce the amount of spam received, and thus potential exposure to viruses and other problems.

For one thing, increasingly chances are that a user's Internet service provider (ISP) is already blocking a considerable amount of spam. Indeed, services such as America Online tout the free spam (and often virus) protection they offer their users. If spam is still getting through, users can set up additional spam blocking either as a feature of a security suite or package or as a separate program. Spam blockers use a variety of techniques to block unwanted messages; the most basic is scanning for certain key words or phrases that are commonly associated with spam. Of course, spammers are always trying to sneak their messages through, such as by misspelling key words.

As with antivirus software, there are also more sophisticated techniques used by spam-blocking software. One is to let the user "teach" the program by identifying some messages as spam. The program will then block messages that contain similar text.

Users can also set up white lists of addresses from which messages should always be accepted and blacklists of sources whose messages should always be blocked. Some antispam software uses constantly updated lists of Internet domains (that is, the part of the e-mail address that follows the @ symbol) from which spam is being sent and blocks all messages from them.

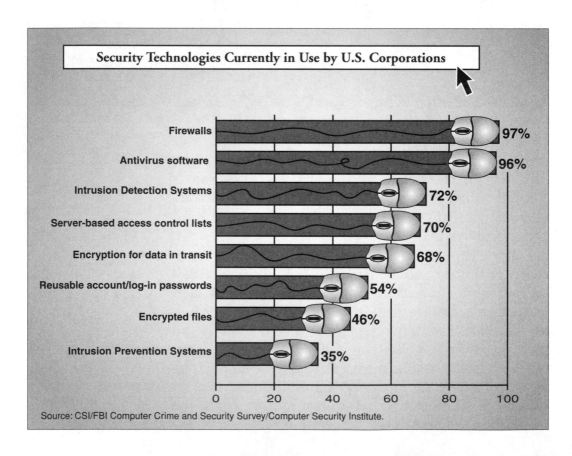

Security Technologies Currently in Use by U.S. Corporations

Firewalls	97%
Antivirus software	96%
Intrusion Detection Systems	72%
Server-based access control lists	70%
Encryption for data in transit	68%
Reusable account/log-in passwords	54%
Encrypted files	46%
Intrusion Prevention Systems	35%

Source: CSI/FBI Computer Crime and Security Survey/Computer Security Institute.

Network-Based Defenses

Beyond the firewalls and other security measures already available to individual PC users, researchers have also been working on programs that could be set up on many computers on the network where they can watch for signs of a worm attack. Worms such as Sasser and Nimda probe for vulnerabilities by sending out requests to connect to the various programs running on the target computer. The monitor program can watch the network for such requests that might identify worm activity.

When a computer receives a request for a service, it sends a reply acknowledging the request. If a monitoring program detects a burst of such replies on the network, this can indicate that worms are present and are bombarding computers with bogus requests.

Monitor programs allow for timely early warning of a cyber attack. As University of Florida computer scientists Shigang Chen and Sanjay Ranka explain: "Once the system is in place and the worm propagation is detected, you can use all kinds of distribution mechanisms to get the alarm out. You can set up subscriptions to distribute the data via e-mail, pagers, newsgroups, or any other existing mechanism."[21]

Caught in the Honeypot

Another way to fight computer intruders is to give them a tempting target, then trap them. This technique, called the honeypot, is sometimes used against hackers. A site filled with intriguing but bogus information is set up and is defended well enough to discourage casual intruders, but not enough to keep out serious hackers. Once a hacker breaks in, his or her electronic moves are recorded and traced. With a little luck, the intruder might be identified, but failing that, at least the hackers have been diverted from attacking real targets.

German researchers led by computer scientist Thorsten Holz have set up a different kind of honeypot

Phishing

A growing form of deceptive e-mail is aimed not at getting people to download viruses, but trying to steal their money or even their identity. This practice, known as phishing, involves sending e-mail that claims to be from a bank or online service. For example, the e-mail may say that the user needs to update his or her eBay or PayPal account because of new security rules.

When the user clicks on the link provided in the e-mail, he or she is taken to what looks like the official Web site for the organization involved. In reality, it is a fake site, and when the user supplies the requested information (such as an account number, credit card numbers, or passwords), the information is captured by the hacker. The information can then be used to access the user's credit or bank accounts and steal money, or even to impersonate the user and create new accounts. (This is called identity theft.)

Recently a stealthier form of phishing has emerged. Its objective is to get the user to click on a link that will download a Trojan horse program. This program installs a keylogger—software that quietly records the user's keystrokes, including account numbers and passwords. This information can then be sent to the phisher's Web site.

Software for identifying and blocking phishing e-mail has been developed, but the most basic defense is for users never to click on Web links found in e-mail. Banks and other institutions hardly ever request user information by e-mail. Users should always access banks and other accounts directly from the Web browser.

system. It creates a system that looks like an ideal target for being turned into a zombie by an intruding worm and allows the attack to apparently succeed. Then, when the hacker's software starts giving orders to the fake zombie, the latter carries them out but also uses them to learn what the hackers are up to, what kind of software they are installing, and what they are doing with the information they are harvesting. If successful, such tactics might be able to turn the tables on the attacker, using the worm's capabilities against its creator.

Virus Research and Response

Despite the best efforts to secure computers, new virus attacks likely will continue for the foreseeable future.

Fighting them requires the coordinated effort and co-operation of both government and private agencies.

Government virus-research efforts center on the CERT Coordination Center at Carnegie Mellon University. It focuses on the technical aspects of attacks, analyzes ongoing threats and trends, and offers technical advice, including emergency help.

A newer organization, US-CERT, was founded in 2003 as the operational arm of the National Cyber Security Division of the Department of Homeland Security. As might be expected, its primary focus is on protecting the nation's critical computer infrastructure from attacks launched by terrorists. In addition to these two CERTs, about 250 other CERT-type organizations currently exist around the world.

This screen displays the Symantec Security Response Web site, which Symantec, an antivirus software company, uses to monitor new viruses and issue alerts to the public.

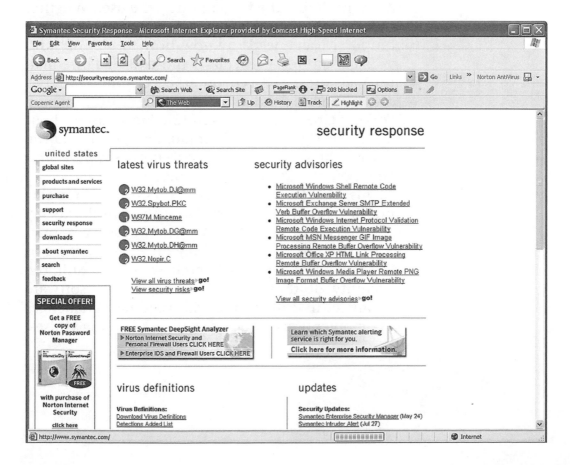

The makers of antivirus software also have an important stake in making sure they can protect their users from viruses. To do so, they constantly monitor the Net for new virus attacks and research them in order to make sure their products can block or eradicate them. An example is the Symantec Security Response Center. Unlike the CERTs, these organizations are focused on the needs of users of particular products, usually for Windows-based computers.

Putting It All Together

Antivirus programs, routers, and firewalls provide defense in depth against viruses and other intrusions. However, the weakest link in computer security is inevitably the human one—the user. Whether at work, school, or home, security experts stress that computer users need to know how to identify and avoid deceptions, particularly those carried by e-mail and Web sites. The Federal Trade Commission and private organizations such as the Anti-Phishing Working Group have worked to educate users about the telltale signs of online fraud, deception, and the downloading of privacy-threatening spyware and other potentially dangerous programs.

Thus, besides using antivirus software, firewalls, and other security measures, security consultants say that users also need to use their heads. A human brain that thinks before clicking on an attachment or Web link may be the final and best defense. Still, the ingenuity of those who write malicious software guarantees that the future will bring new challenges to computer users and those who are fighting viruses.

Chapter 7

Viruses and the Future of Computing

Like everything else in computing, viruses and the techniques for fighting them are both evolving rapidly. It is impossible to say for sure what tomorrow's viruses will look like or to know what techniques might work best in fighting them. However, there are several interesting trends that might provide clues about the future and suggest ways in which the struggle against viruses might influence the further development of computer technology.

Faster and Deadlier

Although the number of different significant viruses has seemingly declined since 2001, the viruses that have shown up in recent years are increasingly virulent. As Peter Tippett, chief technology officer of TruSecure Corporation noted:

They are coming faster. When we had [the] Friday the 13th and Form [viruses], it took a virus two to three years to go from birth to being No.

"A virus ate my homework."

1 [in reported attacks]. Then, when the macro virus Concept came along, it took two to three months. Last year [2001], Nimda took 22 minutes to go to No. 1.[22]

Vincent Weafer, senior director of Symantec Corporation, a leading virus fighter, points out that the threat is not just the faster spread of viruses, but their ability to launch more than one type of attack: "With the worm Nimda, there were multiple payloads—not just data destruction but also creating vulnerabilities and exploiting them."[23]

Modern viruses and worms are often programmed to look for a number of different ways to get into a target system. This means that if one vulnerability (such as in a Web server) is patched, the malware might exploit the Web browser instead or even use e-mail. Further, many worms and viruses are being constructed as blended threats. Future malware is likely to combine features of worms and viruses and use payloads of spyware and Trojan horse programs to gather more information about potential targets.

Bulletproofing the Net?

The creation of more sophisticated, larger-scale attacks suggests that the biggest battle in the war against viruses may be yet to come. Technology executive Richard Ford says:

> Sometime in the next five years, we will see a major outage of at least one service—for example, e-mail or the Web—or one part of the Internet due to malware. The Internet is a lot more fragile than we sometimes think it is. We should think carefully about the different ways the Internet in general could be attacked and design around them.[24]

Advocates of a redesigned Internet point out that the network was never designed to deal with people or things that are not what they appear to be. The presumption has been that a data packet is serving a legitimate purpose and that it should be directed swiftly to its intended destination.

In general, in an Internet designed to be more secure, users and their data would have to be checked before transmission. Today it is easy for a sender of e-mail to disguise or hide his or her true identity and location. However, researchers note that it would be possible to require that all users identify themselves through encrypted certificates and that all messages would be stamped with that identification. E-mail servers would accept only authenticated messages.

Proponents of such a system suggest that it would block virtually all spam, phishing e-mails, and e-mail-borne viruses because anyone who attempted to send such e-mail could be identified and prosecuted. Similar measures could also be used to control the distribution of software and other files over the network.

Such proposals have their critics, however. For one thing, hackers have proven very adept at cracking each new security measure. If new systems give a false sense of security, critics contend that users would be likely to be less vigilant than they are today. The result could be that deceptive messages that do get through might be more likely to be opened, accomplishing their malevolent purposes.

Further, a system that requires that all users and their data be identified would remove the ability to communicate anonymously over the Internet. Much of the fun of using chat rooms and other online social meeting places is the ability to try out new identities, to pretend to be someone else. If people know that anything they say can be traced back to them, they may be afraid to criticize government officials whose actions they disagree with. An even more serious concern is that the ability to be anonymous has proven to be vital for corporate whistle-blowers and others who would be in danger of retaliation from powerful interests.

Two important values are thus in conflict. On the one hand, identifying and authenticating each Internet transaction might greatly reduce the spreading of malware and other criminal activities. On the other hand, an Internet that is too tightly locked up might lose much of its social value as a public forum.

Cyber Vigilantes

In looking at future trends in viruses and computer security, it is also important to consider social trends and how they might affect the use of technology. Societies respond to the threat of crime and disorder in different ways. The Internet is often considered to be the frontier of the twenty-first century. Like the

A Lot of Bots

Bots (short for *robots*) are programs designed to run autonomously, carrying out tasks such as searching the Web for information, helping shoppers find the best prices, or entertaining chat room users with humanlike conversations. Well-designed bots (sometimes called intelligent agents) can be a useful part of the Internet world.

Recently, however, virus writers and spammers have been reported to be using armies of bots in their shady activities. First they use special software to scan for vulnerable machines and install bots on them. The bots listen for commands, which they can receive through a variety of channels, including chat rooms. The bots can then be directed to attack other computers, plant viruses or Trojan horses, steal information, or send spam.

Unfortunately, bots are harder to detect and remove than worms. Unlike worms, which tend to blunder about, leaving data trails behind, bots are designed to be stealthy. A bot may patiently wait or probe only a few systems at a time, so it transmits few suspicious data packets over the network.

Recently whole networks of coordinated bots (called botnets) have been encountered. A botnet can be commanded to launch a denial-of-service attack against a Web site or to send a flood of spam that cannot be traced to a single point of origin. It is even possible for a botnet to be used to combine the processing power of thousands of systems into a virtual supercomputer that could be used to crack encrypted passwords and raid bank accounts.

Bots, viruses, and worms live in what biologists would call a symbiotic relationship. Viruses or worms can plant bots, which in turn can distribute more viruses or worms.

nineteenth-century frontier of the Wild West, the Internet has relatively little regulation. Under such conditions, residents of cyberspace sometimes feel the need to act directly against criminals.

Some computer security experts have decided that it is not enough to respond passively to virus or worm attacks or even to build better defenses. Tim Mullen, Information Technology director for AnchorIS, an accounting software firm, says, "I was looking at all the things I had to secure against, all the things I had to pay for, and I got fed up with it. I decided to take matters into my own hands."[25] In 2002 Mullen

IT security consultant Tim Mullen developed a program that attempts to halt the spread of worms by backtracking and blocking them at the source.

released a demo version of a program that would target worms such as Nimda, which had attacked many Microsoft Windows systems the previous year.

If a computer protected by Mullen's software were to be sent a copy of the Nimda worm, for example, the computer would "pretend" to be vulnerable to it, but, when the worm attempts to install its "hook" into the operating system, Mullen's program sends special code of its own back to the attacking computer. This code uses the same means to enter the attacking computer that had been used by the original worm, and then inserts a block that prevents that computer from spreading the worm further. If applied widely enough, this mechanism would halt the spread of the worm.

While Mullen's demonstration was interesting and harmless, some experts worried that other versions of counterstrike software could be as dangerous as the original virus or worm. For example, a program that responds to a virus attack by cutting off the Internet access of the attacker could bring down an innocent (though infected) online business.

Many experts therefore worry about an escalation of online conflict and do not support the idea of creating good viruses to fight bad ones. Besides shutting down innocent computers that have been taken over by the enemy virus, the good virus itself might have a flaw that causes it to spread through the Internet, slowing down or damaging millions of systems.

One alternative is a program that takes the middle position—it merely patrols rather than responding, so it does not become the equivalent of an armed vigilante. One example of such a program is iSIMS, from a company called Symbiot; iSIMS quickly analyzes an attack while it is ongoing. It identifies the type of virus, worm, or hacking intrusion and reports to the client's system administrator the likely effect on a company's computers. A program like iSIMS gains much of its strength from the fact that all the computers running the software are linked, so they can compare notes in real time.

After analyzing the type and extent of the attack, iSIMS offers a number of suggested responses—but leaves it up to the client to decide what to do. The responses can range from simply blocking or slowing down traffic from a site identified as the source of the attack or diverting the attack by creating a fake site (honeypot). Attacking hackers can also be tagged so other computers will recognize them as attackers, or their attacks can even be reflected back at the originating computer.

Critics still worry that even Symbiot's program goes too far, but the company defends its product, saying that the more extreme measures would only be used if all else failed and a business or other organization was truly being destroyed by an attack. As for the innocent computers that might be targeted by retaliatory measures, Mullen and Symbiot both believe

Although computer programmers are developing a kind of digital immune system for computers of the future, antivirus software currently offers the best protection against viral attack.

that users who refuse to take basic precautions such as installing antivirus software and a firewall are at least partly responsible for what might happen. In their view, such careless users should share some of the consequences as well. As with the fight against street crime, there are no easy answers, although some experts suggest that it would be better to focus on a patient, sustained effort to build more secure systems and to strengthen laws and law enforcement.

Fighting Viruses with Simulations

While cyber vigilantes are controversial, many researchers agree that it is not enough simply to react to new viruses and try to contain the damage. They say that this guarantees that virus fighters will always be on the defensive. The alternative is to be proactive —to try to predict what future attacks might look like so defenses can be prepared ahead of time.

At the CERT Coordination Center, computer scientist David Fisher is developing Easel, a simulation program that uses data from real attacks to create simulations of devastating attacks that may come in the future. Sam Curry, a virus expert at McAfee Software, notes, "We can't hope to stop them, but by knowing what might happen when they do hit, we can at least keep them contained."[26]

A Digital Immune System

Researchers have often pointed out the similarities between computer viruses and their biological equivalents. These similarities suggest that a computer might someday be able to fight computer viruses in a way analogous to the way the immune system in the human body deals with microscopic intruders. When an unknown microorganism enters the human body, antibodies recognize that the invader does not belong. The immune system then tailors antibodies to deal with the particular infection. Thus, while it usually takes a few days of misery, healthy people can fight off colds or the flu. Perhaps, researchers say, computers could fight off infections in the same way.

In 2000 IBM and Symantec began to develop a system based on an idea proposed in 1992 by researchers Stephanie Forrest and Alan Perelson. So far they have created simulations that suggest that a digital immune system is possible.

The system would work like this: When a computer virus is encountered by a computer equipped with the special software, the infected file is sent to a central computer for analysis. This computer is connected to a special isolated network that allows the virus to execute its code. This network tries to identify what the virus needs in order to reproduce and offers it, triggering the virus to demonstrate its infectious behavior.

Analyzing the code and behavior of the virus, the digital immune system creates a signature, or unique set of data that can be used to identify the virus "in

Viruses, Worms, and Artificial Life

Like their biological counterparts, computer viruses and worms seem to be somewhere on the borderline between nonliving and living. A virus can reproduce only with the aid of a host user. However, some of today's sophisticated computer worms can not only reproduce, seeking "food" in the form of computing resources, they can even communicate with one another. In other words, they are beginning to act more like animals than like things.

Meanwhile, since the 1980s researchers have tried to create computer programs that share many of the characteristics of living things. This includes the ability to learn. Neural network programs consist of many small parts that attempt to carry out a task, such as recognizing a picture. The parts that are most successful are reinforced in much the same way as the human brain forms new pathways as a task is learned.

Researchers have also created genetic programs that contain bits of program code that represent different ways of solving a problem. The programs that are most successful are allowed to reproduce, combining their digital genetic code with other successful programs. Surprisingly effective programs have resulted from such artificial evolution.

If computer worms were given features such as neural networks and genetic code, the result might be robust, constantly evolving creatures for whom the Internet is as natural an environment as a plain or forest is for animals. However, responsible researchers would want to be very careful about such experiments. Advanced forms of artificial life, constantly evolving and adapting, might be very hard to eradicate.

the wild." It also creates an antidote—for example, it might create a patch that would block requests coming from the virus. After the signature and antidote are tested to make sure they work with the virus, they are sent to all the other computers that subscribe to the service. This means that the computers are now in effect inoculated against the virus. Although this technology is experimental, by 2005 Symantec and other companies were already starting to incorporate it in products designed to protect large corporate networks.

Despite the fact that computers continue to fall prey to viruses, increasingly sophisticated antivirus software is minimizing the threat of attack.

An Uncertain Future

As both those who create viruses and those who write antivirus software continue to develop new capabilities, the war against viruses is likely to be open-ended. There will certainly be new attacks—quite possibly serious ones. In 2003, the twentieth anniversary of the first network virus, Simon Perry of Computer Associates said that he was "confident therefore . . . that within [twenty years] an attack that we would today classify as warfare or terrorism that includes a cyber element is a certainty."[27]

Another expert, Graham Cluley of Sophos, a major antivirus company, agreed that the threat of future attacks is real, but he tried to put it in perspective:

> We'll see more viruses undoubtedly. There is no such thing as a usable virus-proof computer system. But anti-virus software is getting better at protecting against new, unknown threats and is using the internet to its advantage. I don't think viruses are going to cause the end of the world but it's not a trivial "fluff on the jacket" problem either. We need to keep the problem in perspective and not panic.[28]

In the long run, the computing community will have to deal with the fact that information systems are vital to the functioning of our economy and indeed, our society itself. In turn, legislators, law enforcers, businesspeople, and ordinary computer users will all have to take responsibility for protecting these critical systems against ever-changing threats. In doing so, people will also have to make sure that the freedom and creativity that has made this powerful and versatile technology possible is also preserved.

Notes

Chapter 1: The Development of Computer Viruses
1. Steven Levy, *Hackers: Heroes of the Computer Revolution.* Garden City, NY: Anchor/Doubleday, 1984, p. 27.
2. Quoted in "Elk Cloner," *Wikipedia: The Online Encyclopedia.* http://en.wikipedia.org/wiki/Elk_Cloner.

Chapter 2: The Worm Turns
3. Quoted in Charles Schmidt and Jim Darby, "The What, Why, and How of the 1988 Internet Worm," The Morris Internet Worm. http://snowplow.org/tom/worm/worm.html.
4. Katie Hafner and John Markoff, *Cyberpunk: Outlaws and Hackers on the Computer Frontier.* New York: Simon & Schuster, 1995, p. 321.
5. Eugene H. Spafford, "Crisis and Aftermath: The Internet Worm," *Communications of the ACM*, June 1989.

Chapter 3: The Viruses Spread
6. Quoted in Chris Taylor, "Attack of the World Wide Worms: How a Series of Prolific Viruses Clogged Computer Networks, Bared the Vulnerability of the Internet and Showed the Cracks in Windows," *Time*, September 1, 2003, p. 48.
7. Quoted in Matt Hines, "Does IM Stand for Insecure Messaging?" CNet News.com, March 23, 2005. http://news.com.com/Does+IM+stand+for+insecure+messaging/2100-7349_3-5629037.html.

Chapter 4: Why Do They Do It?
8. Quoted in Leslie Brooks Suzukamo, "Online Security Threat Evolves: Computer Viruses Give Way to Phishing, E-mail Scams," *St. Paul Pioneer Press*, February 6, 2005, p. D1.
9. Hafner and Markoff, *Cyberpunk*, p. 11.

10. Quoted in Steven Levy, "Biting Back at the Wily Melissa: A Sneaky E-mail Virus Invades Thousands of Computers, Leading to a Worldwide Cyberhunt and a Quick Arrest," *Newsweek*, April 12, 1999, p. 62.
11. Jon Katz, "Who Are These Guys?" *Time*, May 15, 2000, p. 53.
12. Quoted in Dan Verton, *The Hacker Diaries: Confessions of Teenage Hackers*. New York: Osborne/McGraw Hill, 2002, p. 20.
13. Quoted in "Sophos Reports on New Spam Tactics and Top Ten Viruses for 2004 in Annual Threat Analysis," Sophos. www.sophos.com/pressoffice/pressrel/us/20041208year topten.html.

Chapter 5: Counting the Cost

14. Quoted in Tim Lemke, "Penalties Stiffened for Identity Theft; New Law Gives Harshest Sentences to Terrorists, Corporate Insiders," *Washington Times*, July 16, 2004, p. C11.
15. "Q&A: How Often Does Virus Hysteria Occur?" Vmyths. com. http://vmyths.com/hoax.cfm?id=258&page=3&cat= Frequently%20Asked%20Questions%20(FAQs).
16. Maryfran Johnson, "Chicken Little Viruses," *Computerworld*, February 19, 2004, p. 20.
17. Quoted in "Good Times Virus Hoax," Hoaxbusters. http://hoaxbusters.ciac.org/HBMalCode.shtml#goodtimes.
18. Quoted in "CIA: Take That, Cyberterrorism!" *Wired News*, May 25, 2005. www.wired.com/news/politics/0,1283,67644, 00.html.
19. James A. Lewis, "Assessing the Risks of Cyber Terrorism, Cyber War, and Other Cyber Threats," Center for Strategic and International Studies, December 2002. www.csis.org/tech/ 0211_lewis.pdf.

Chapter 6: Fighting Back

20. Becky Worley, *Tech TV's Security Alert: Stories of Real People Protecting Themselves from Identity Theft, Scams, and Viruses*. San Francisco: Tech TV, 2004, p. 106.
21. Quoted in Ryan Naraine, "Researchers Propose Early Warning System for Worms," eWeek, April 20, 2005. www.eweek. com/article2/0,1759,1788294,00.asp.

Chapter 7: Viruses and the Future of Computing

22. Quoted in Gary H. Anthes, "Malware's Destructive Appetite Grows: Viruses, Worms and Trojan Horses Will Become More Powerful, More Pervasive and Faster," *Computerworld*, April 1, 2002, p. 46.

23. Quoted in Anthes, "Malware's Destructive Appetite Grows."

24. Quoted in Anthes, "Malware's Destructive Appetite Grows."

25. Quoted in Barbara Moran, "Vigilantes on the Net: When Laws Fail and Enforcement Won't Work, Desperate Citizens May Be Tempted to Take Matters into Their Own Hands," *New Scientist*, June 12, 2004, p. 26ff.

26. Quoted in Kevin Hogan, "Worm Watchers: Simulation Tools Fight New Network Parasites," *Technology Review*, January/ February 2002, p. 24.

27. Quoted in Will Sturgeon, "The Virus at 20: Two Decades of Malware," Silicon.com, November 11, 2003. www.silicon.com/software/security/0,39024655,39116851, 00.htm.

28. Quoted in Sturgeon, "The Virus at 20."

Chronology

1949   Mathematician John von Neumann develops the idea of storing programs in memory. This is the basis for modern digital computing and, potentially, for viruses and worms.

1960s   Early self-styled hackers explore computers.

1969   The first computers are connected in the network that would eventually become the Internet.

1979   Researchers at the Xerox Palo Alto Research Center develop the first network worms to perform useful tasks.

1982   A fifteen-year-old creates Elk Cloner, the first personal computer virus. It runs on the Apple II.

1983   Fred Cohen, a University of Southern California graduate student, creates networked computer viruses as an experiment.

1984   *Scientific American* describes the game Core Wars, where programs compete in the arena of computer memory.

1986   The first virus for the IBM PC, Brain, is written by two Pakistani programmers.

1988   Robert T. Morris Jr. unleashes the Internet worm, which infects about six thousand computers.

1994   The Good Times e-mail virus hoax, although harmless, demonstrates how easy it is to trick users into opening message attachments.

1995   The Concept virus is the first to use Microsoft Word macros, showing how viruses can be embedded in documents attached to messages.

1999   The Melissa virus uses e-mail to spread rapidly among millions of Internet users, causing an estimated $80 million in damage.

2000   The Love Bug virus uses the words "I love you" in an e-mail subject line to entice users into opening an attachment and spreading the infection; the first wave of distributed denial-of-service attacks is launched from virus-controlled zombie computers, temporarily shutting down numerous Web sites, including Yahoo!, eBay, and Amazon.

2001   The Code Red and Nimda worms spread rapidly.

2003   The innovative Sobig family of worms uses Web sites to download updated instructions.

2004–2005   Worms and viruses are used to spread spam containing deceptive phishing messages.

Glossary

antivirus program: A program or set of programs designed to identify, disinfect, or block viruses or worms.

attachment: A file such as a document or graphic that accompanies an e-mail message. Attachments are a common way of spreading viruses.

back door: A function that allows direct control of a program by bypassing normal security. Back doors are sometimes accidentally left in programs and later exploited by hackers.

black hat: A hacker term for a hacker who puts his or her skills to criminal uses such as stealing credit card numbers.

bot: Short for *robot*, a program that pursues its goals without human supervision. Bots can have beneficial uses but can also be planted by viruses to launch attacks on Internet sites.

botnet: A group of bots distributed around the Internet but coordinating their efforts, such as for a Web site attack.

code: Program instructions written in a special language such as C or Visual Basic.

Computer Emergency Response Team (CERT): One of a number of agencies dedicated to responding to computer attacks. The official government-sponsored CERT is at Carnegie Mellon University.

denial-of-service attack: The jamming of a Web site with information requests, blocking it from access by users.

Distributed Denial-of-Service (DDOS) Attack: A denial-of-service attack launched by a large number of computers that are under the control of a worm or virus.

encryption: Changing text or program code into a form that cannot be recognized without being processed (decrypted) using a key word or phrase.

exploit: A specific technique that takes advantage of a particular vulnerability on an operating system or software program.

firewall: Software (or a hardware device) that blocks dangerous or inappropriate data packets on the Internet.

hacker: Originally, an obsessive, highly skilled explorer of computer capabilities; later, the term came to be associated with computer break-ins and the creation of viruses.

identity theft: The assumption of a person's identity, usually for the purpose of gaining access to cash or credit.

infection: A virus that is actively running or ready to be triggered, such as by rebooting the computer.

infector: The mechanism by which a virus spreads, such as by finding e-mail addresses and mailing itself as an attachment.

logic bomb: A destructive program set to be triggered on a certain date or following a specified event. Logic bombs can be planted by some viruses.

macro: A set of instructions for an applications program such as a word processor. Macros can be included in documents and run when the document is opened. Macros can contain virus code.

malware: From "malicious software," this is a general term for viruses, worms, spyware, and other harmful or intrusive programs.

payload: The instructions that a virus carries out after it has reproduced—for example, deleting files on the hard drive.

phishing: The use of deceptive e-mail to trick the reader into clicking onto a link, such as for eBay or PayPal. The link actually connects to a fraudulent site that looks like the real one. Information provided by the user is then used to steal money from bank or credit card accounts.

polymorphic virus: A virus that can modify its own code (such as by encryption) to make it difficult for antivirus programs to identity it.

script kiddie: A hacker term for an inexperienced, often young, hacker who must use scripts created by someone else.

social engineering: A hacker term for techniques used to trick computer users into giving information or access to their systems. E-mail-borne viruses depend on social engineering to be able to spread.

trigger: The code in a virus that determines when it will carry out its payload instructions.

Trojan: Named for the Greek horse, an innocuous-looking program that contains a virus.

virus: A program that can modify other programs or parts of the operating system in order to reproduce itself and possibly cause damage.

virus hoax: A false warning about a virus; it can waste time or conceal a real virus.

virus scan: Systematic checking of all files on a computer for possible viruses. This is a basic feature of antivirus programs.

white hat: A hacker term for someone who uses hacking skills primarily to gain knowledge or to discover and fix vulnerabilities.

worm: A program that can make copies of itself, often spreading across a network. Like viruses, worms can contain damaging payloads.

zombie: A computer that is being used by a virus, such as for Web attacks—usually without the knowledge of the machine's owner.

For Further Reading

Books

Peter H. Gregory, *Computer Viruses for Dummies*. Hoboken, NJ: Wiley, 2004. Provides user-friendly advice on how to use antivirus software, guard one's PC from infection, and deal with any viruses that get through.

Katie Hafner and John Markoff, *Cyberpunk: Outlaws and Hackers on the Computer Frontier*. New York: Simon & Schuster, 1995. Presents vivid accounts of the exploits of hackers and the underground computer culture in the early 1990s.

Steven Levy, *Hackers: Heroes of the Computer Revolution*. Garden City, NY: Anchor/Doubleday, 1984. A fascinating narrative history of the early hackers who obsessively explored computers and created many of the software tools still in use today.

Ed Tittel, *PC Magazine Fighting Spyware, Viruses, and Malware*. New York: Wiley, 2004. Includes detailed reviews and recommendations for antivirus software, personal firewalls, spam blockers, and other tools for protecting one's PC.

Dan Verton, *The Hacker Diaries: Confessions of Teenage Hackers*. New York: Osborne/McGraw Hill, 2002. Presents vivid accounts of young hackers—how they became involved with hacking, the decisions they made, and the consequences.

Becky Worley, *Security Alert: Stories of Real People Protecting Themselves from Identity Theft, Scams, and Viruses*. San Francisco: Tech TV, 2004. The author includes interesting stories and useful practical advice for protecting oneself from online dangers and securing one's PC.

Periodicals

Gary H. Anthes, "Malware's Destructive Appetite Grows: Viruses, Worms and Trojan Horses Will Become More Powerful, More Pervasive and Faster," *Computerworld*, April 1, 2002.

Barbara Moran, "Vigilantes on the Net: When Laws Fail and Enforcement Won't Work, Desperate Citizens May Be Tempted to Take Matters into Their Own Hands," *New Scientist*, June 12, 2004.

Chris Taylor, "Attack of the World Wide Worms: How a Series of Prolific Viruses Clogged Computer Networks, Bared the Vulnerability of the Internet and Showed the Cracks in Windows," *Time*, September 1, 2003.

Tom Zeller Jr. and Norman Mayersohn, "Can a Virus Hitch a Ride in Your Car?" *New York Times*, March 13, 2005.

Internet Sources

John Lasker, "U.S. Military's Elite Hacker Crew," Wired News, April 18, 2005. http://www.wired.com/news/privacy/0, 1848,67223,00.html.

Robert Lemos, "Alarm Growing over Bot Software," ZDNet. com, April 30, 2004. http://news.zdnet.com/2100-1009_ 22-5202236.html.

———, "Spam May Sprout Viruses in Home PCs," CNet News.com, June 27, 2003. http://news.com.com/2100-1009 -1021636 .html.

Declan McCullagh, "Spying on the Spyware Makers," ZDNet.com, May 4, 2005. http://news.zdnet.com/2100- 1009_22-5694727.html.

Web Sites

CERT Coordination Center (www.cert.org). Originally founded as the Computer Emergency Response Team in 1988 and based at Carnegie Mellon University, this organization provides descriptions of attacks, trends, and technical advice.

CNET.com (www.cnet.com). A good source of news, technical help, and software reviews for PC users.

Cybercrime Knowledge Center (www.computerworld.com/ securitytopics/security/cybercrime). This site, sponsored by *Computerworld* magazine, includes a variety of background materials and news reports on criminal use of computers, including new forms of virus and hacking attacks.

Electronic Frontier Foundation (www.eff.org). A civil liberties organization for the information age, the EFF opposes some security measures that might restrict the ability to use the Internet freely and anonymously.

Electronic Privacy Information Center (www.epic.org). Provides resources and advocacy for the privacy of computer users. Includes materials on spyware and other online threats.

Federal Trade Commission (FTC) (www.ftc.gov). The FTC provides warnings about online scams and fraud such as phishing e-mails.

Hoaxbusters (http://hoaxbusters.ciac.org). Part of the problem with viruses is that it is often difficult for users to know which threats are real and which are nonexistent or at least exaggerated. The Hoaxbusters site describes a variety of Internet hoaxes (including warnings about nonexistent viruses) and explains how to identify them.

Works Consulted

Books

John Biggs, *Black Hat: Misfits, Criminals and Scammers in the Internet Age*. Berkeley, CA: APress, 2004. Offers portraits of and interviews with actual online hackers, criminals, and people working on the margins of the law.

Dorothy E. Denning and Peter J. Denning, eds., *Internet Besieged: Countering Cyberspace Scofflaws*. New York: ACM, 1998. A collection of technical, legal, and social policy articles focusing on how to design the Internet so it will be more resistant to hacker attacks.

Steve Furnell, *Cybercrime*. Boston: Addison-Wesley Professional, 2001. Describes the growing activities of hackers, including system intrusions and viruses, and the response of the government, the media, and the public.

David Harley, Robert Slade, and Urs E. Gattiker, *Viruses Revealed: Understand and Counter Malicious Software*. New York: Osborne/McGraw Hill, 2001. Provides extensive background and technical discussion of all forms of viruses, worms, and related software.

Yvonne Jewkes, ed., *Dot.cons: Crime, Deviance and Identity on the Internet*. Portland, OR: William, 2003. A collection of essays on ways in which a variety of computer criminals challenge the rules of society.

Peter Lilley, *Dot.con*. Sterling Page, VA: Kogan Page, 2002. Explains how computer systems are compromised and exploited, including the use of viruses as a tool for online fraud.

Paul R. MacDougall, ed., *Overview of Computer Fraud and Abuse*. Hauppage, NY: Nova Science, 2002. Describes the provisions of the federal Computer Fraud and Abuse Act, which can be used to prosecute creators of viruses and worms.

Kevin D. Mitnick and William L. Simon, *The Art of Deception: Controlling the Human Element of Security*. Indianapolis, IN:

Wiley, 2002. Mitnick, an infamous but now reformed hacker, explains how users are tricked into allowing access to their computers and other facilities.

———, *The Art of Intrusion: The Real Stories Behind the Exploits of Hackers, Intruders and Deceivers*. New York: Wiley, 2005. Mitnick changes his focus from deception to the use of hacking techniques to exploit system vulnerabilities, including the planting of Trojan programs. Each scenario is followed by recommendations for prevention.

Michael Newton, *The Encylopedia of High-Tech Crime and Crime-fighting*. New York: Checkmark, 2004. This A to Z guide has entries for types of computer crime, hackers, high-tech criminals, and many famous computer viruses and worms.

Eric S. Raymond, *The New Hacker's Dictionary*. 3rd ed. Cambridge, MA: MIT Press, 1996. A fascinating compilation of the unusual words, phrases, and concepts used in the hacker culture. The emphasis is on the original, creative hackers rather than modern computer vandals and cyber-criminals.

Tsutomu Shimomura and John Markoff, *Takedown: The Pursuit and Capture of Kevin Mitnick, America's Most Wanted Computer Outlaw—By the Man Who Did It*. New York: Hyperion, 1996. Another classic tale of hackers and their pursuers, but this one is controversial because Mitnick and a number of hackers dispute some of the facts.

Bruce Sterling, *The Hacker Crackdown: Law and Disorder on the Electronic Frontier*. New York: Bantam, 1992. Although not specifically about viruses, this book gives an interesting account of the first major crackdown against hackers and the concerns it raised about the rights of Internet users.

Clifford Stoll, *The Cuckoo's Egg: Tracking a Spy Through the Maze of Computer Espionage*. New York: Pocket, 1990. Classic tale of how an astronomer inadvertently became a computer security expert when he discovered a seventy-five-cent discrepancy that had been caused by a mysterious hacker.

Synovate, *Federal Trade Commission—Identity Theft Survey Report*. McLean, VA: Synovate, September 2003. Presents statistics on the frequency and impact of identity theft and related crimes.

Douglas Thomas, *Hacker Culture*. Minneapolis: University of Minnesota Press, 2002. Explores the history of the hacker subculture, hackers' images of themselves, and the changing popular image of hacking.

Periodicals

Celeste Biever, "Following the Trail of the Zombie PCs," *New Scientist*, March 26, 2005.

Kevin Hogan, "Worm Watchers: Simulation Tools Fight New Network Parasites," *Technology Review*, January/February 2002.

Jon Katz, "Who Are These Guys?" *Time*, May 15, 2000.

Tim Lemke, "Penalties Stiffened for Identity Theft; New Law Gives Harshest Sentences to Terrorists, Corporate Insiders," *Washington Times*, July 16, 2004.

Steven Levy, "Biting Back at the Wily Melissa: A Sneaky E-mail Virus Invades Thousands of Computers, Leading to a Worldwide Cyberhunt and a Quick Arrest," *Newsweek*, April 12, 1999.

Maryfran Johnson, "Chicken Little Viruses," *Computerworld*, February 19, 2004.

Jonathan Littman, "The Shockwave Rider," *PC/Computing*, June 1990.

Eugene H. Spafford, "Crisis and Aftermath: The Internet Worm," *Communications of the ACM*, June 1989.

Leslie Brooks Suzukamo, "Online Security Threat Evolves: Computer Viruses Give Way to Phishing, E-mail Scams," *St. Paul Pioneer Press*, February 6, 2005.

"A Thousand Ills Require a Thousand Cures: Researchers Are Borrowing from Immunology to Improve the Security of Computer Networks," *Economist*, January 8, 2000.

Internet Sources

"CIA: Take That, Cyberterrorism!" *Wired News*, May 25, 2005. www.wired.com/news/politics/0,1283,67644,00.html.

Fred Cohen, "Experiments with Computer Viruses." www.all. net/books/virus/part5.htm.

Michelle Delio, "Find the Cost of (Virus) Freedom," *Wired News*, January 14, 2002. http://wired-vig.wired.com/news/print/ 0,1294,49681,00.html.

"Elk Cloner," *Wikipedia: The Online Encyclopedia.* http://en. wikipedia.org/wiki/Elk_Cloner.

Federal Bureau of Investigation, "2004 CSI/FBI Computer Crime and Security Survey." http://i.cmpnet.com/gocsi/db_area/ pdfs/fbi/FBI2004.pdf.

"Good Times Virus Hoax," Hoaxbusters. http://hoaxbusters. ciac.org/HBMalCode.shtml#goodtimes.

Matt Hines, "Does IM Stand for Insecure Messaging?" CNet News.com, March 23, 2005. http://news.com.com/Does+ IM+stand+for+insecure+messaging/2100-7349-3_5629037.html.

Patricia Keefe, "Virus Alerts Run Amok," *Computerworld*, March 18, 2002. www.computerworld.com/securitytopics/security/ story/0,10801,69160,00.html.

James A. Lewis, "Assessing the Risks of Cyber Terrorism, Cyber War, and Other Cyber Threats," Center for Strategic and International Studies, December 2002. www.csis.org/tech/0211_lewis.pdf.

Ryan Naraine, "Researchers Propose Early Warning System for Worms," eWeek, April 20, 2005. www.eweek.com/article2 /0,1759,1788294,00.asp.

Scarlet Pruit, "Hackers Plot More Phishing, Mobile Viruses," *Computer"world*. www.computerworld.com/securitytopics/ security/cybercrime/story/0,10801,101325,00.html?SKC= cybercrime-101325.

"Q&A: How Often Does Virus Hysteria Occur?" Vmyths.com. http://vmyths.com/hoax.cfm?id=258&page=3&cat= Frequently%20Asked%20Questions%20(FAQs).

Charles Schmidt and Jim Darby, "The What, Why, and How of the 1988 Internet Worm," The Morris Internet Worm. http://snowplow.org/tom/worm/worm.html.

Sophos, "Sophos Reports on New Spam Tactics and Top Ten Viruses for 2004 in Annual Threat Analysis." www.sophos. com/pressoffice/pressrel/us/20041208yeartopten.html.

Richard Stiennon, "Threat Chaos: Making Sense of the Online Threat Landscape," Webroot Software. http://i.i.com.com/ cnwk.1d/html/itp/WP_Threat_0305.pdf.

Will Sturgeon, "The Virus at 20: Two Decades of Malware," Silicon. com, November 11, 2003. www.silicon.com/software/security/ 0,39024655,39116851,00.htm.

Web Sites

Anti-Phishing Working Group (www.antiphishing.org). This organization conducts research and promotes public awareness about phishing, or the use of deceptive e-mails and Web sites. Phishing can be used to spread viruses or obtain information for use in identity theft.

Association for Computing Machinery (www.acm.org). A major organization for computer scientists. Provides a huge library of resources, including news and papers on computer security topics.

Microsoft (www.microsoft.com). Includes software updates, security patches, and alerts for Windows users.

Symantec Security Response Center (http://security response.symantec.com). Provides information about current virus threats and other security risks for Microsoft Windows systems.

US-CERT (www.us-cert.gov). This Web site is sponsored by a division of the U.S. Department of Homeland Security and focuses on protecting vital infrastructure from potential computer-based terrorist attacks.

VMyths.com (www.vmyths.com). The VMyths site is another useful resource that describes virus hoaxes in general as well as having an A to Z listing of specific examples.

ZDNet.com (www.zdnet.com). Another excellent source for PC-related news, technical help, and software downloads.

Index

ActiveX, 61
antivirus programs, 46, 73–74, 82–85
Apple II, 25
applications, 24–25
artificial life, 106

binary numbers, 15
black hats, 11, 63
Blaster worm, 51, 59
botnets, 101
bots, 101
Brain virus, 27–28
Bropia worm, 52
Brunner, John, 29
Bush, George W., 72

cell phones, 52
central processing units (CPUs), 20–22
chat rooms, 62–63
Chen, Shigang, 93
Cluley, Graham, 108
Code Red worm, 41, 70
Cohen, Fred, 22
computer attacks, 9, 68–71, 77
  see also viruses; worms
computer culture, 9–10, 62–63
Computer Emergency Response Team (CERT), 9, 37, 95
computer epidemiology, 54–56
Computer Fraud and Abuse Act, 39
computer memory, 15
  buffers, 34, 86–87
  multitasking and, 20–22
computer networks, 29–30, 86, 90
  see also Internet
computers, 7, 9, 12–16, 38
  see also personal computers (PCs)
Core Wars (game), 22
Curry, Sam, 105
cybercrime

hackers and, 65–67
economic costs of, 68–70
identity theft, 7, 66–67, 71–72
laws against, 48–49
vigilantism and, 100–104
cyber terrorism, 78–81, 108

Defense Advanced Research Project Administration, 37
denial-of-service (DoS) attacks, 71, 101
Dertouzos, Michael, 53
Deutsch, Peter, 18–19
Dewdney, A. K., 22
Digital Equipment Corporation (DEC), 16–17
digital immune systems, 105–107
disk operating system (DOS), 24–25

Easel, 105
Eckert, John Presper, 14
Elk Cloner, 25–26
e-mail
  attachments, 9, 43–46
  authentication of, 99–100
  phishing, 66–67, 94
  spam, 65–67, 90–92
encryption, 28
ENIAC, 13–15
ethics, 10, 38

finger utilities, 34
firewalls, 87–90
Fisher, David, 105
Ford, Richard, 99
Forrest, Stephanie, 105

Genocide2600, 64–65
Good Times virus, 75–76
gray hats, 11, 65
Guzman, Onel de, 48–49

Hackers, 18–20, 57–60, 64
  alienation of, 61–63
  black hats, 11, 63
  crime and, 65–67
  gray hats, 11, 65
  white hats, 11, 18, 63
Hackers (film), 64
Hafner, Katie, 37, 60
Hall, Jeff, 60
Hepps, Jon, 29
hoaxes, 74–76
Holz, Thorsten, 93–94

IBM PC, 27–28
identity theft, 7, 66–67, 71–72
instant messages (IMs), 52
intelligent agents, 101
Internet, 40, 99–100
iSIMS, 103

Johnson, Maryfran, 75

Katz, Jon, 62
Kelvir worm, 52
keylogger software, 94
Kuo, Jimmy, 52

lamer, 18
leet, 18
Levy, Steven, 19–20
logic bombs, 77
Love Bug virus, 48–49, 70

macros, 44
mainframe computers, 15–16
malware, 7, 97–99, 106–108
Markoff, John, 37, 60
Massachusetts Institute of Technology
  (MIT), 18–19
Mastoras, Greg, 65
Mauchly, John, 14
Melissa virus, 43–48
Microsoft Windows, 41, 51, 61
minicomputers, 16–18
Mitnick, Kevin, 10, 11
monitor programs, 93
Morris, Robert Tappan, Jr., 35–37, 39
MS-DOS, 27
Mueller, Robert, 81–82
Mullen, Tim, 101–104

Netnews, 32
Nimda worm, 41, 70, 98, 102

Olsen, Kenneth, 16–17
online culture, 9–10, 62–63

Parson, Jeffrey Lee, 59–60
PC-DOS, 27
PDP-1, 16–17
Perelson, Alan, 105
Perry, Simon, 107–108
personal computers (PCs)
  early, 24–28
  worms and, 40–42
phile, 18
phishing, 66–67, 94
ports, 86

Ranka, Sanjay, 93
Redcode, 22
Rheingold, Howard, 32
routers, 88–89

script kiddies, 57–60
security measures, 11, 20, 90, 92–93, 96
  antivirus programs, 82–85
  cost of, 73–74
  counterstrike software, 101–104
  cyber terrorism and, 78–82
  digital immune systems, 105–107
  e-mail authentication, 99–100
  firewalls, 87–90
  future trends in, 99–108
  honeypot systems, 93–94
  patches, 86–87
  simulations, 105
  spam blockers, 90–92
sendmail, 34
September 11, 2001, 11
Serflog worm, 52
service packs, 87
Shock, John, 29
Shockwave Rider (Brunner), 29
simulations, 105
SirCam worm, 70
Skrenta, Richard, 25
smart homes, 54
Smith, David L., 47–48
Smith, Richard, 46–47
Sober worm, 76

Sobig.F worm, 41–42
software, 12–15, 19–20
    counterstrike, 101–104
    time-sharing, 19–21
    vulnerabilities in, 9, 86–87
software piracy, 26
Spafford, Eugene, 38–40
spam, 65–67
spyware, 55
SQL Slammer worm, 41
Sudduth, Andy, 30
Suriv-02, 28
Symantec Security Response Center, 96
Symbiot, 103–104

terrorist attacks, 11, 78–81, 108
Tippett, Peter, 97–98
Trojan horses, 9, 52, 53
TX-O microcomputer, 19

UNIVAC, 15
Unix, 22–23, 32–35
US-CERT, 95
Usenet, 30, 32
U.S. military, 76–77

vampire worm, 29–30
VicodinES virus, 47
virtual communities, 32
viruses, 7–9, 12–15, 20–22, 44, 52

counterstriking, 101–104
economic costs of, 68–70
in e-mail attachments, 9, 43–46
future trends in, 97–99, 106–108
hoaxes, 74–76
prevalence of, 70–71, 73
research on, 54–56, 94–96
as weapons, 76–77
Web site attacks by, 50–51
Vmyths.com, 75
von Neumann, John, 14, 15

warez, 18
War Games (film), 64
Weafer, Vincent, 51, 98
Welchia, 35
white hats, 11, 18, 63
wireless security, 90
World Wide Web (WWW), 40
Worley, Becky, 82–83
Worms, 7, 15, 33–35, 93, 106
    on early networks, 29–30
    future trends in, 97–99, 106–108
    on the Internet, 30–33, 35–39
    new generation of, 41–42
    study of, 54–56

Xerox Palo Alto Research Center, 29

zombie computers, 51

Picture Credits

Cover: Victor Habbick Visions/Photo Researchers, Inc.

© A. Huber/U. Starke/zefa/CORBIS, 67; AP Wide World Photos, 17, 36, 47, 49, 59, 62; © Bettmann/CORBIS, 14, 25; Chris Hondros/Getty Images, 40; © CORBIS SYGMA, 64; Courtesy of Tim Mullen, 102; © Claudius/zefa/CORBIS, 8; © David Brown/Cartoon Stock, 58; © David Cooney/Cartoon Stock, 54; Greg Pease/Getty Images, 38–39; © Harley Schwardon/Cartoon Stock; © J BOUNDS-RNO/CORBIS SYGMA, 10; © Jerry Cooke/CORBIS, 13; Joe Raedle/Getty Images, 104; © John Pritchett, 33; Lisa Terry/Liaison/Getty Images, 21; Lester Lefkowitz/Getty Images, 80; Lucas Schifres/Landov, 107; Maury Aaseng, 44, 45, 50, 61, 69, 71, 79, 87, 92; Mike Mergen/Bloomberg News/Landov, 83; © Noel Ford/Cartoon Stock, 98; Prestige Newsmakers/Getty Images, 23; © Roger Ressmeyer/CORBIS, 27; Symantec Corporation, 84, 95; The U.S. Department of Energy's Computer Incident Advisory Capability (CIAC), 74; Time-Life Pictures/NASA/Getty Images, 31

About the Author

Harry Henderson is a graduate of the University of California, Berkeley. He has written numerous books on science, technology, and public policy issues for adults and young people. His computer-related books include *The Encyclopedia of Computer Science and Technology, Privacy in the Information Age*, and two Lucent titles: *The Internet* and *Issues in the Information Age*. He lives in El Cerrito, California, with his wife, Lisa Yount, also a prolific writer, artist, and crafter.